"GETTING THE BAND BACK TOGETHER"

"GETTING
THE BAND
BACK TOGETHER"

How a Band of Renegades REDISCOVERED
Their Lives and Gained Total FINANCIAL &
TIME FREEDOM in Less Than 36 Months.

DR. DAVID PHELPS, DDS

EPI
MEDIA
Rockwall, Texas

Dedicated to Robert "Dr. Banjo" Porter
September 11, 1954–September 7, 2021

Until we get the band back together Bobby, play on my friend!

Table of Contents

Introduction

It all started with a Christmas letter. In the winter of 2021, Dr. David Scharf sent me a letter of gratitude, wherein he wrote:

Dear Kandace and David

Please forgive the formality of a typed note, but if I wrote it by hand you could never read it.

2 hours ago I closed on the sale of my practice. Karen and I cried for half an hour. What an emotional experience. I felt the weight of the world come off of chest. I called my parents, my kids, my siblings and some close friends. I wanted to sit down and express my appreciation to you.

I never would have gotten to this point without Freedom Founders. You helped me realize that I had more than enough money for the rest of my life and I could take my foot off the gas and start to enjoy myself.

I will still be practicing a few days a week by choice. As I have told you in the past, once I had the realization that I didn't need to earn another dollar to live the rest of my life, I began to enjoy practicing more then ever. No more of the worries that go along with practice, just seeing patients and getting the joy that comes from helping others. My gift is helping people in the way that I do and I'm not wanting to give that up now.

What will I do with my newfound freedom? My hobby has always been drumming. I reached out to some old band mates and we are commencing rehearsals next month. Hopefully we will start playing out in the spring. I have been a volunteer fireman for almost 20 years now but never had the time to move up the leadership ladder. I now have the freedom to pursue that passion as well.

I wish you both all the blessings of the Christmas season and a happy and healthy new year.

Best regards

Dr. Scharf and I had spent the year, off and on, working toward his freedom. He's a periodontist who spent all his time working with his hands, managing his business, and worrying about it around the clock, but he was so much more than that. He was a husband, a father, an active member of his community, and—long ago—even a drummer in a band. But most of his time was taken up by his practice—until it wasn't.

A few months after he and I started working together, Dr. Scharf began to have more free time. His mind began to fill with exciting possibilities: Could he and his wife enjoy traveling and spending more time together? Could he provide a lasting legacy for his adult children? Could he get the band back together?

I've written before about my own story—how, mid-career, I confronted the very same transition from active income to passive cash flow. You may know the story of my daughter's leukemia and life-saving liver transplant, the long recovery she had, and the role those played in my own transition from full-time practice work to freedom.

But my story isn't the only story. In fact, in the years since I started Freedom Founders in 2010, I've encountered dozens of business owners and practice owners who had stories that blew me away. Stories that made my eyes misty and my heart beat twice as fast. Stories of pain, redemption, determination, frustration, and ultimately, yes, sweet freedom.

Finally feeling free upon the sale of his practice, Dr. Scharf wrote: "What will I do with my newfound freedom? My hobby has always been drumming. I reached out to some old bandmates and we are commencing rehearsals next month."

Dr. Scharf is just one of fourteen contributors featured in this book. Each one has worked to achieve freedom, finally earning the time to, metaphorically, "get the band back together." You'll hear from Drs. Gertrude and Bob Dubanski who overcame wrist injuries that left their practice floundering; Dr. Dennis and Monzell Perry, who, mid-career, lost their savings to bad investments; and Drs. Peter and Janice Farrehi, who discovered freedom meant they had time to invest in a long-term independent living community for their adult son on the autism spectrum.

The stories of these practice owners and business owners who achieved freedom are important for many reasons, but most of all, I hope, because they're similar to yours. You may be like many of the business owners I meet—struggling with work, frustrated by lack of time, wondering if pulling back from the grind will ever be realistic.

In writing this book, it's my hope that you see yourself in these stories. You see the beginnings of a change that can happen. You see that the obstacles around you are less intimidating, find the walls less formidable, and discover your own courage and resourcefulness are more than enough. After all, our time is more precious than we ever know.

Time—We Can't Buy It Back

I never played in a band, but I find the metaphor of "getting the band back together" fits so much of what's best about freedom.

On September 7, 2021, one of my best "bandmates"—a deep, lifelong friendship that never changed over time—passed away from COVID. It was unexpected. It shouldn't have happened. In my opinion, it wasn't his time.

Once again, my own mortality and those of whom I care most were brought right back to the surface. Bob and his family grew up not more than thirty minutes from my home and yet I didn't prioritize the time that I should have to bless our relationship.

Bob Porter ("Dr. Banjo") and I sat side by side in our dental school lecture halls and laboratories for four consecutive years. We also waited tables on nights and weekends to help defray the cost of our education. Let's just say that we knew each other at a pretty deep level.

Bob loved music and played guitar, banjo, ukulele, and probably a host of other instruments. This was his side gig and love (second only to his love of the Lord, his wife, Nancy, and his two adult sons, Bobby Jr., and Josh). The leader of our band has died, but that band will be getting back together again in due time.

I've dedicated this book to Dr. Bob Porter and the impact that he had on so many people over his lifetime. Perhaps it can help promote his legacy going forward.

If you're reading this book, you likely have the means, however unlikely it seems now, to change your circumstances. Freedom is here, ready for you, not far down the road—sometimes, it's just around the corner. But you don't have much time (if any) to lose.

To make a great change, all we need is a story to inspire us and a guide to show us that the path ahead is more doable than we feared.

Little Hinges Swing Big Doors—A Small Mindset Shift That Changes Everything

Being of the mindset that finances and financial planning are too complex for the busy business owner or professional is a myth that has been sold to the majority. As a result, the majority achieve less than stellar results over time and often wonder "where all the money went" over the three to four decades that most work to grind out a living.

Making money is what we are taught to do, but there is a limit to how much we can make. It's a hamster wheel with no end in sight.

Making our money work as hard for us as we did for it is not taught in 99 percent of the academic educational programs today. It becomes a major inflection point for those who invest the time to become skilled in this regard. Learning how to do this is best done through self-education and by surrounding oneself with entrepreneurs on the frontier of creating their own freedom in life.

The Ultimate Denominator of Wealth Is TIME

It doesn't matter how much you amass in your 401(k). If you can't access it until 59.5 years of age, you will find yourself stuck behind the chair until that date. I speak with many practitioners who have been disciplined to save and invest enough to retire in their late 40s or early 50s, only to realize that their options to enjoy that freedom are limited because they can't access any of that hard-earned money for years. They find themselves stuck behind the chair, having earned enough to buy their freedom but being unable to use it.

If your money is not enabling you to buy back your time, then of what use is it, really?

If your money is not enabling you to buy back your time, then of what use is it, really? The ultimate denominator of wealth is time.

The 'Do or Die' Cyclicality of the Markets—There's Got to Be Another Way!

The real tragedy of the $12 trillion that has been erased from the global markets in the volatility we experienced throughout 2021–2022 is the lost TIME that it represents. One of our newest members confided in me that he had lost $800k on Wall Street in the six months before joining Freedom Founders. How many years will it take him to re-earn that wealth behind the dental chair? Do you really want to bet the future years of your life on this game?

Not only time and money, but peace of mind. The contrast between the two approaches was striking at a member event in early 2022. While the sky was falling in the traditional markets, our members were calm, confident, and grateful. No fear. No running for the exits. No watching the financial news feed every hour.

What was the difference?

There Is No Magic Bullet—There Are Only Fundamentals

My good friend Alastair MacDonald spent years as a guide in the jungles of Africa. At age nineteen, he won a coveted contract to guide National Geographic in some of the most remote regions of the world.

In the jungle, what you don't know can kill you. To journey without a guide would be stupid and deadly. But for a guide who knows how to identify threats, like how to read the swish of an elephant's tail to avoid trouble, the risks can be mitigated and the journey becomes an adventure of opportunities.

The same holds true in the marketplace. One of the best things that I did when I was young, with more enthusiasm than smarts, was to connect with old-timers who knew real estate like the back of their hands. These mentors took me under their wing. They helped me avoid a thousand threats I never knew existed and set me on the road to success.

Admittedly, in my younger years, I learned some lessons the hard way and have the scar tissue to prove it. But the older I get, the more valuable it becomes to me to avoid wasting time wandering paths alone when I can follow the trail of an experienced guide.

Unlike financial advisors who have a vested interest in maintaining your ignorance (their job security—"pay no mind to the man behind the curtain"), a guide is someone who has gone before and who wants to show you the way. The best guides in my life have been those who have accomplished what I wanted to accomplish, and who desired to show me the way.

To be clear, I don't expect my guides to have a "perfect" track record; far from it. The best learning experiences are usually marked by scars.

What I look for in a guide:

- **Full Cycle Experience:** No fair weather experts who put out shingles when the weather is sunny and the markets are rising. I want someone who has had experience when the hammer drops.

- **Integrity When It Hurts:** Things don't always go according to plan. Nothing in life is guaranteed. What matters is how you respond to challenges. Integrity means standing fast; communicating early, often, and clearly; owning up to mistakes; and taking care of those for whom you bear responsibility.

- **A Maverick Mentality:** The courage to question "conventional wisdom." There are many really smart people who are still beholden to society's definition of success. I'm looking for people who are willing to take ownership of their life, not blindly accept the value system they've been taught by peers, colleagues, or society at large.

Today, my network of contrarians (Freedom Founders) is my best insurance policy. That is the only "magic bullet" that has preserved tens of millions in wealth while Wall Street burns.

My advice?

- Be willing to question conventional financial wisdom
- Beware the madness of the crowds (irrational exuberance)
- Focus on fundamentals
- Find a guide (or better yet, a community of advisors)

And remember: Your network is your net worth.

As Dr. Scharf enjoys the freedom that allows him to reconnect with himself, the people, and the endeavors he loves, let us also strive for that same freedom.

It's time we, too, get the band back together. So dust off your guitar, plug in your amps, call your buddies and let's rock on. Freedom calls.

It's time we, too, get the band back together.

Yours in Freedom,

David Phelps, July 2022

CHAPTER 1

DR. DAVID AND KAREN SCHARF

When I was in my mid-thirties, with more than a decade of hard work at my periodontist practice under my belt, I decided to invest my entire savings—seven figures—with a financial advisor specializing in private loans. Within a year, all my money was gone.

I was devastated. I felt bad for my own stupidity. The advisor had been recommended by a friend and we trusted him, but I didn't know enough about investing. In hindsight, I realized that my own greed had motivated me, negatively, to pursue such a risky avenue for my hard-earned money.

For a long while, I couldn't help but wonder: *What would that money have been worth when I was in my sixties? What would it have meant for my family had I not thrown it away on bad investments?*

The worst part, though, was how the loss affected my approach to work. Naturally, I'm a saver. So, after losing it all, I made up my mind that I would hunker down, work as hard as I could, and save.

The downside? I got stuck in this go-go-go mode for decades because I just couldn't work hard enough to make up for having lost that money. I put my hobbies on the back burner; my youthful passions fell by the wayside.

Things weren't all bad, though. I had a very successful Long Island-based periodontist practice—super busy, super profitable. No complaints there, except I never knew how much was enough—or if tomorrow it was all going to fall apart.

I have three kids—Baylee, Samantha, and Jonathan—today ranging in ages from 23 to 30. I worked hard, put my kids through school, and went on vacations. All in all, it was a good life.

When it came to our money, I played it safe. I kept it in a basket of index funds, which meant that when downturns like the 2008 Great Recession happened, I wasn't too worried. Over the decades, I saw a steady, minimal rise, with no worries about any volatility along the way. Playing it safe was important for another reason, too; I invested my personal money in the same place where we invested our practice's retirement plan money. As I had a fiduciary duty to my employees, we kept the volatility to a minimum.

Traditional Retirement Strategies Were All We Knew

My wife Karen and I never really talked about retirement money. That's because our approach was the norm—I'd work and save until I didn't have to anymore. Then I'd retire and we'd live off the standard 4 percent per year, hoping we didn't outlive our money.

While that may be the norm, it never felt right to me. It's like eating a cow versus milking a cow. Doesn't it make more sense just to milk it and live off that?

In the back of my mind, I've always admired people who invest in real estate. They seem to be well off and appear to have a lot of free time. That said, as I had a full-time job as a dentist and no mentors in my circle to show me how to invest, I never had the time or know-how to do it right. In other words, my first step into real estate wasn't pretty.

About six years ago, I had some extra money I wanted to invest, so I bought a small commercial building near my office. I liked the area and my real estate agent liked the deal. That should've been enough, but it turned out to be another disaster.

What I didn't know was that the property was zoned in a way that the local village board had to approve any new tenant, and this approval procedure took three months, minimum. So imagine a prospective business's surprise when they find this place that they like and it takes three months to find out if they've been approved or not. Why put up with the hassle?

At one point, the property sat vacant for a year. When I bought that building, I didn't know what I didn't know. Eventually, I just decided to sell it, take my lumps, cut my losses, and be done with it. We found a buyer and she signed the contract. The day after signing, the buyer was doing the contracted walk-through of the building, found asbestos, and backed out. I immediately offered to remediate the asbestos at no cost to the buyer. There was a lot of back and forth, tying up the building for a while, but finally, I sold the building to a different buyer—an asbestos remediation company! They bought the building, became the perfect tenant, and I took my lumps. At the end of the day, I broke even between the depreciation and the total rent.

I had thought I was generating a cash cow. But, looking back, I just had no idea what I was doing. I was learning at the school of hard knocks, which can be very expensive. Fast forward to the summer of 2020. I'm scrolling through Facebook, and I see some posts from David and Freedom Founders.

COVID Had Crippled My Business and I Was at the End of My Rope

This was the first summer after the COVID shutdown, which had been a super stressful time—closing the practice, reopening with new protocols, managing our staff. In many respects, I was burned out.

David's message couldn't have arrived at a better time: *Do you have enough money to retire? If you retire now, what do you want to do?*

After calls with David and Alex at Freedom Founders, I dipped my toe into joining by first signing up for the education modules. I wanted to review the training they'd put together on real estate. After watching all the videos over one weekend, I was hooked. I liked the whole concept they spoke about, and I liked that they were teaching me what to do—not doing it for me. In that moment, I decided to join, which turned out to mark the beginning of a new chapter in my life.

By that point, I had enough money saved up that I probably could have retired anyway and not worked. I wasn't relying on my practice income coming in every day to live on. But I always felt that the practice had a fragility to it, even though I probably had the most respected practice on Long Island. I was busy, had a great staff, and everything was good, but I always sort of felt like, "Better get it while the getting is good, because it could all end tomorrow." COVID only made that feeling all the more real for me. I always worked hard, because you never knew what tomorrow may bring. COVID validated this feeling. While the practice may sometimes feel like a locomotive, barreling down the tracks, in reality, it could always stop on a dime. Stuff can always happen. This feeling sent me searching for something else to do; a way to generate money without having to work.

That November 2020, Karen and I did a virtual Blueprint Day with David and Kandace. We enjoyed it because we could lay out all our assets and goals and get a sense of whether or not it was enough. I realized I had more than enough, even without touching my retirement plan money. I could just use the money that was non-qualified to generate income.

The Blueprint gave us direction in terms of how we should deploy our funds, how much we could draw, and more. By the time we finished, I had a clear direction on what to do and how to deploy our funds. From there, it just became a matter of talking to the Trusted Advisors, doing the paperwork, and getting started.

I had a lingering hesitancy, just because of the bad investment I'd endured early in my career, but Freedom Founders was totally different. David's whole approach is about education. He has created a walled garden, where the people you deal with are honest and vetted. Sure, there's always the chance that a deal may go bad, but it's never because you're dealing with a dishonest or incompetent person. I think back to the commercial real estate I bought, and the real estate agent I worked with who helped me buy the property. Had I been working with a real estate agent of David's caliber, they would've told me in advance, "Hey, do you realize the local village rules require a three-month review period before approving a tenant?" That's the type of make-or-break insight you get only when you really trust who you're working with.

Your Network Determines Your Net Worth

Now I'm plugged into a network. I have dozens of different people I trust in this network who approach me for various deals.

Because we know each other well, we can move so much faster. At the same time, we have savvy lawyers well-versed in ironing out details. So if a friend needs a favor—say, to take over an investment because he needs to cash out early, and I can get a 20 percent return in two months—then I can say yes to such a deal and not needlessly worry about all the little details.

I've learned the value of plugging into that network and working with these trusted people. Plus, that two-month deal paid my annual Freedom Founders dues! Real estate can be extremely profitable, but only when you're plugged into a network that supports you.

Sure, Freedom Founders is not a small investment to join, but I came to the realization that I would lose at least that much money if I tried to get the education on my own. So why not afford myself the education and not lose that money? Now I have a network of vetted troubleshooters. It's a tremendous thing.

When it comes to investments, I enjoy learning about them. It feels exactly like spending time with a hobby. Dentists make a living with their hands like we're carpenters. To be able to make a living with my mind is fantastic. Making a decision about what generates income, passively, is the epitome of fun.

For years, my practice was a monster. It's still a monster, but I'm now experiencing financial freedom because my passive income provides me enough cash flow to live on should I fully retire.

I don't need to practice anymore. I don't need to keep my foot all the way down on the accelerator every single day. I don't need to work like a dog. Having this newfound freedom gave me the clarity to realize I don't need to work so hard.

I was probably in Freedom Founders for less than a year when one day I started reviewing the spreadsheet where I track my money coming in every month. As I'm looking at it, I suddenly realize that the money coming in every month from Freedom Founders is enough. It's enough to live off of for the rest of our days. Anything more that I make in the practice is just gravy; I could sell it and be just fine. I don't need that extra income.

Everything in a practice is your responsibility, from the equipment breaking to worrying if you're going to have a HIPAA or OSHA complaint, staff issues, tax issues—you name it. It falls on your shoulders. On the days and nights when I wasn't working in the practice, these responsibilities were always on my mind. I was constantly worried about the practice.

For me, the first step toward freedom was being able to sell my practice. I didn't want to stop practicing because I did enjoy the dentistry side, which I do three and a half days a week. But I was happy to let go of all the other responsibilities.

Now, I'm still working about the same as before, but I'm thinking about patients, not business-side issues, like upgrading my file server, replacing broken equipment, or updating payroll forms. I just come in, do the job I love, and leave when my patients leave.

Before, it was very hard to be present. I'd be with my kids when they were young, but my mind would be on something else. It was hard to be totally focused on what I was doing because I was worried about something with the practice.

Freedom Founders helped me realize that I don't need my practice anymore. Now I can be present when I'm not working. I have more time for myself where I'm not distracted. It's life-changing.

Freedom Allowed Me to Live Again

My second step into freedom was picking up some things that had fallen by the wayside. I play the drums, so I started playing in the band again. We're a bunch of hack musicians who jam out to the rock music we grew up with—Mustang Sally, the Beatles,

Creedence Clearwater Revival, Neil Young, Cream, R.E.M.—the classics. I played with these guys fifteen years ago, and then just fell out of doing it.

The guys had reached out to me a few years ago. They were getting the band back together and wanted me on drums, but I just had too much on my plate at the time. We just restarted in January 2022. We do gigs. We need 30–40 songs to play a whole gig, so we make time to practice. It's nice to play out, from time to time. Mostly I just enjoy going out with my friends and doing our thing. I'm just happy to get together once a week and jam for a few hours.

When you're playing music, you can't think about anything *but* playing music. It's really relaxing because with almost anything else you can do—exercising, driving, watching TV—your mind wanders. Your mind doesn't wander playing music.

I remember the first time I played out and got paid. It was only about $10, but it was still the most amazing thing to get paid for playing the drums. It was such a small amount of money . . . but I felt exhilarated.

I've been a volunteer fireman for six years, but now I have the freedom to get more involved. We have a vacation house, and so I'm active with the fire department in June, July, August, and September when we're there. That's also when the majority of the calls come in. As a volunteer fireman and EMT, we get about 250 calls in those four months. Aside from the calls, there are other ways I'm looking to get involved, such as fundraising.

In addition, I always wanted to be more involved in our synagogue. I've been on the board of directors for a couple of years, but I would temper how much I would be involved because of the time I could commit. At most, they needed the website to be done, so I took over that project, hired the person, and did the website. But we have more time to commit, so we can finally be more involved.

DR. DAVID AND KAREN SCHARF

I've also made more time for myself. Now, every day I exercise. I make time to meditate. I go into the little home sauna we have, and I spend more time with my wife. I've peeled off more time for us to be able to relax and do the things that we want to do.

She, too, has more time. She was incredibly involved with the business side of the practice. She'd handle the nuts and bolts of all the staff forms, the payroll, and more.

I could never have run the practice without her help. She never complained about it, but she hated it. She did it because it was our business and she wanted to help me, but let me tell you: today, she doesn't have to do those things anymore, and she's so happy.

Freedom Founders has me looking forward to my future with joy. Within the group, I really like the members we have. I've met a lot of people who I just enjoy connecting with. I enjoy being plugged into the network. I enjoy being Free for Life™ and the advanced education we get. I enjoy speaking with David and the others who help us learn so much, and I enjoy paying it forward as a FIT Captain.

FIT Captains are the veteran members who lead the Freedom Implementation Teams. These are the small pod groups of Freedom Founders members who meet weekly virtually to discuss wins of the week, update on current activities and goals, discuss investing strategies, and share resources.

When I started at Freedom Founders, we had some really good FIT Captains and leaders who shared so much time and were an invaluable resource to me and the other newbies. I try to emulate those leaders to make it a good experience for the new members of my group.

For me, the biggest freedom is peace of mind. That peace of mind has two parts. First, it's about not constantly having to worry about the practice. Second, it's about controlling my future. I'm not subject to whether the stock market is up or down or what income

I'm going to make in the office. Instead, I can use my money to generate money. At the same time, I can live the way that I want to. I'm in control of my own money, making the decisions for how that money is going to generate cash flow, and enjoying the education that precedes making good decisions. And I can plug into an organization of top people willing to provide invaluable guidance. It's the best of all worlds.

If I could sum it up, the most precious gift of freedom is freedom from worry. A friend of mine once said, "Worry is a debt that can never be paid." The freedom to be present and not worry is akin to playing in the band. My mind isn't preoccupied. I can just enjoy the company of those around me and focus on making music.

Karen's Insight & Observation

When we were in our 30s, David and I invested with someone, and we lost a tremendous amount of money. So when David started looking into Freedom Founders, I thought, *"oh no. Here it goes again. We can't go through this again."*

But fast forward two years . . . Since David sold the practice and joined Freedom Founders, his stress level has been significantly lower. He spends more time with us. He's gone on trips with the kids. He is much more present when he is home. It used to take him hours to decompress after coming home at the end of the day. He was so wound up. Life is different now.

Today, he is so much more relaxed. He has time again. We just took our first 3-week vacation. We've never done that before—we're able to do that without worrying about anything.

GETTING THE BAND BACK TOGETHER
DAVID'S TAKEAWAYS:

Dr. David Scharf was the inspiration for this book. His Christmas letter to Kandace and me in December 2021 became the basis for the title.

The turning point for the Scharfs was their Blueprint Day, which demonstrated they had more than enough assets to provide for their lifestyle after practice once they re-deployed that capital into cash flow-producing assets.

With freedom in sight, Dr. Scharf got his band back together. With his newfound freedom and time, he renewed his old bandmate friendships and set up a new rehearsal schedule! Additionally, his new freedom opened up the opportunity to pursue a greater leadership role as a volunteer fireman.

Freedom from worry about not having enough allowed David and his wife, Karen, to travel at will and to involve his three adult children in the principles of Freedom espoused by the Freedom Founders community, including family investments into real estate opportunities. This is what generational legacy is all about!

CHAPTER 2

DR. JAMES AND SARA GREEN

"Thankfully, you have plenty more time to work. So just keep on working, keep doing what we tell you, and it'll all be okay."

That's the "advice" my stockbroker gave me in 2008 when decades of our investments crashed and we were faced with starting over. At the time, I was mid-career, and not ready to retire. I was content to continue working but I knew I couldn't work forever. And something about this advice to "just keep working and keep doing what we tell you" didn't sit right with me.

I'm a general dentist. Up until recently, we had one practice and our life revolved around work and family. Sara, my wife, has an MBA and was our marketing director. We have one grown son, Zachary, who's also in business, and based in Dallas. We're very family oriented, with my sister and sister-in-law living close by, along with lots of nieces and nephews. We value our family time on the weekends and family trips.

By 2018, our life was good, but we had uncertainty. What was our retirement going to look like? Financially, we would be depending on our money in the stock market and retirement plan vehicles. When we looked at the future, we didn't think we had saved enough. *Am I still gonna have to work for decades more?* I wondered.

Sure, Sara and I had done some alternative investments, real estate, and different venture capital opportunities, but we were primarily in the stock market. We had gone through the big crashes of 2000 and 2008 while investing with big stockbroker companies, with less than stellar results.

At the same time, we have friends who are older than us, who had worked hard and retired with a nest egg invested on Wall Street. When the 2008 Great Recession hit, they were back at work, only six months after celebrating retirement. Some of them are still working to this day, fifteen years on! They can't afford not to, having lost everything in the stock market after relying on brokers and other people to look out for them. That reality was scary for us.

I enjoyed working, so I didn't have an urgent need to walk away, but I did realize that I couldn't work forever. After watching others my age develop health problems and back problems, I didn't want to be that person who was stuck full-time because they have to be.

Sara and I would talk about our future a lot. We've always had open communication in our relationship. We share our stresses and what's on our minds. But up until we joined Freedom Founders, Sara pretty much left the financial stuff up to me, as far as managing the stock market and dealing with brokers and investments.

I Was Craving Community . . .

So I had been going it alone for years, and in many ways, I was craving a community. Even when I did investment deals with friends, which worked out fine, in many respects it still felt like I was working alone.

I first heard about David Phelps and Freedom Founders through a couple of friends who had gone into alternative investments like real estate. I listened to some of David's recordings and read the blogs, and I really liked what I heard, because it was a whole different way of thinking.

Putting most of my money in the stock market had always made me feel uneasy. Meanwhile, everything David said made sense. On top of that, when you have a group of people as we do at Freedom Founders who are all involved in alternative investing *together*, then you have a network of people supporting you and that you can rely on. They help you vet deals, which is a huge difference maker, and that's really what appealed to me. I have opportunities to invest in different things through friends or connections and have a whole community helping to make sure that those deals work out.

Our son and I went to our first meeting, which was in Dallas. There we met a lot of people and quickly realized *these people are just like us*. Sara was skeptical like many spouses would be. Like, *What are you going to get us into next?*

But she went with me to the next meeting in San Diego, and within the first half day, she looked me in the eye and said, "This is where we belong." I was feeling the same thing. There, at that meeting, we felt like we had finally found a home.

Everybody at the meeting was very open and friendly. All

> . . . she looked me in the eye and said, "This is where we belong." I was feeling the same thing. There, at that meeting, we felt like we had finally found a home.

the presentations were upfront and easy to understand, and every topic made sense. What mattered most to us was hearing from all the other couples who were practice owners—doctors, dentists, orthodontists, attorneys; all different types of people. Everybody there was open to being learned from, welcoming, and eager to share their stories about why they were there and how their investments were going.

Sara and I had been to a few other professional meetings where attendees were very competitive. We've also had a couple of bad experiences in other meetings that turned out to be a pitch for flimsy investments.

As Sara puts it: "We were a little skeptical, which is pretty normal. Because, many times at these other events, the pitches sound very good, but they're actually not. In this case, personally, I was very impressed. I got the sense that Freedom Founders was absolutely the right thing to do for the two of us. And we walked away from that first meeting incredibly excited."

I know Sara to be a smart and savvy businesswoman, so for her to know very quickly that Freedom Founders was the real deal meant a lot to me. We both found the Freedom Founders experience to be extremely refreshing.

From that San Diego meeting, there were several takeaways we wanted to act on right away. First, we had so much to learn. Both Sara and I started soaking up information like water from a fire hose.

"James had always been the one who took care of all the business decisions. I knew what was going on, but I was never fully involved. When I left San Diego, I was impressed that everybody in the room really knew what was happening with their investments. I realized I didn't have much knowledge, so it became very important for me to learn as much as I could."

Second, the idea of freedom became a motivating force in our life. As Sara tells it: "I know how hard James works, taking care of work and making investment decisions. He was working so hard, but we never had a clear path to get to a place of peace, where we could enjoy life. So I think that freedom—the word itself, *freedom*—really made a huge impact on us. We wanted the freedom that was within reach."

Soon after San Diego, in December 2019, we did our Blueprint Day with David and Kandace at their home in Dallas. That was an eye-opening experience. We like to think we are very organized, hard-working people who pay attention, but having someone on the outside look at what we were doing—and not just financially— was enlightening.

For most of my time as a practicing dentist, I was the do-it-all owner, doing everything for everybody. The business couldn't function without me, and I don't say that with pride. Both Sara and I were doing everything for the business by ourselves. The Blueprint Day showed us how to move away from the markets and redeploy wealth into things like a self-directed IRA, but it also showed us how to free up more time, immediately.

First, David introduced us to the work of Gino Wickman, founder of the Entrepreneurial Operating System (EOS). Applying what we learned from EOS helped us reorganize our management and took a lot of stress off of us personally. Sara became the implementer of the EOS, which means she ran the office. Second, we brought on a consultant, recommended by David, who helped us restructure our business's financial structure.

The timing couldn't have been better. We started our business overhaul right at the end of February 2020, and over the next six weeks into April, as our practice remained closed due to the lockdowns of the COVID pandemic, we retrained all our employees over Zoom calls. We held meetings the whole time and completely reorganized the business, management, and accountability structure of the office. We came out of lockdown very strong.

The Community Provided Wisdom during COVID to Stay Grounded and on Track

With Freedom Founders, we also had weekly meetings to go through resources and help each other get through the new regulations to minimize the hits to our businesses during the COVID lockdown. There are many things that make being a member of Freedom Founders worthwhile, but having that community's guidance and friendship during lockdown made it completely worth it.

We then got our investor badges, which you achieve after completing a series of introductory training modules about alternative investing. These modules provide the basis of the initial education required before a Freedom Founder member may begin making investments through the curated opportunities in the network of the community.

As 2020 marched on, we went through the process of moving money into self-directed plans, liquidating assets, and changing our mindset to prioritize cash flow from passive income. Thus far, it's worked out beyond our highest expectations.

Sara: "The first few months, there's just so much information. You get to meet all of the different Trusted Advisors (TAs), each one of them fascinating in their own right. With the abundance of great information, you wonder, *how do I make sense of all of this?*

"We did a lot of listening. Listening to the TAs, listening to the members—listening to what they're doing, what their goals are, what they're learning. Nobody was pushy. Everybody was happy

18

to share. We didn't redeploy our wealth in the first month, but we were learning as much as we could."

Then, after about five or six months, as we started to see the same folks at meetings and on calls, and as those folks became friends, everything began to click. Truly, as David says, "Your network is your net worth." Freedom Founders is a network-building organization—one that David has built and helped shepherd very carefully.

With our office restructuring in place, we found ourselves with far more time on our hands. At first, we spent quite a bit of time building our network, studying the investments, learning the process, and thinking about a future beyond the practice.

Personally, now that I have a lot more time, we are slowly but surely starting to enjoy it. First, we added an outdoor kitchen area to our house and redid the backyard. Second, we were able to take off on Fridays. We had always been at the office on Fridays doing paperwork, but now? We're at home or doing what we want to do, with no paperwork in sight. We now have the time to just do normal life stuff rather than trying to squeeze everything into a Friday afternoon or after 6:00 pm during the week.

> *. . . now that I have a lot more time, we are slowly but surely starting to enjoy it.*

With the business side taken care of, the other doctors and I focus exclusively on the patients, and normally we're through by 3:30 in the afternoon. On Thursdays we're usually done by 2:00. We've shortened the number of hours in our workdays and the number of days in our work week while actually producing *more* dentistry than we were before because we're more efficient.

Our next step with Freedom Founders is to officially become Free for Life™, which is when we've replaced the active income we need for our lifestyle with passive income, plus a 20 percent safe harbor to handle the unexpected. We've already redeployed our assets and submitted the paperwork to become Free for Life™, so the celebration is on the horizon. But I can write with confidence that this is a huge deal for us.

A couple of years ago, I had zero confidence that I could walk away from my career and be okay. Today, I know that if we didn't want to go to the office anymore, we wouldn't have to. We have options—great options—that give us peace of mind and, most importantly, freedom.

Freedom Founders has us thinking of assets in terms of cash flow rather than as piles of money subject to the volatility of the stock market. Freedom Founders has also opened up a whole different world of communication because it's more of a couple's participation; it's designed for spouses to participate together. Today, we're more collaborative in our decision-making; Sara's involved in all of our investing and really understands how the money part works.

As Sara tells it: "James was constantly thinking, 'Oh, my goodness, what is the market doing? This is horrible!'" The stock market is honestly very scary because so much is outside of your control and that's the opposite of how we're invested now. Which is 100 percent in our control. We make the decisions, and it's huge."

By actually sitting down together, determining how much money we spend, how much to invest and reinvest, and what our budget was, we started to feel in control. We started doing this during our Blueprint Day and it's what helped us later arrive at our freedom. We now have a true Freedom Number™—the monthly passive cash flow that exceeds one's monthly living expenses. Once that number is achieved, that person qualifies for Free for Life™ status within the

Freedom Founders community. We live the life we want to live, but with our eyes open and both of us on the same page.

I've always looked at success from several different standpoints. First is in caring for our family, where everyone is healthy, educated, and taught how to be well. Second is success in dentistry, in the service we provide for our patients. The third is financial success, which means our finances help us achieve our goals of spending more time with our family.

Freedom Felt Illusive and Out of Reach

Over the years, I didn't feel like I had the freedom to leave; now I do. If I take a day or a week off, I know that it'll be okay. We're able to take time off and still maintain our responsibility to care for our employees, patients, practice, family, and everything else.

Now I get to play golf two or three times a week. I have time to just take the day and drive out to the farm to hang out with my brother-in-law, who's a farmer. I grew up on a farm and ranch, and I missed that life for a long time because I felt like I had to work non-stop. I also read a lot more. For probably eight to ten years, I didn't read a whole lot. I would buy the books—I've got stacks and stacks—but now I'm finally working my way through them because I can actually sit on the patio for a few hours and enjoy reading.

As Sara tells it, "To have the time and the freedom to spend time with family is a huge thing. We are also active in mission trips, where we take time to give back."

Sara founded a nonprofit organization fifteen years ago called Latin Gala Charities. Its goal is to help people in need from El Salvador, Colombia, and Nicaragua—where Sara is originally from—by connecting them to other local nonprofits that provide financial support. Then, during the pandemic, when we were unable to continue doing the fundraising events, we instead spent our time helping out at the food bank; with organizations at school; and with local nonprofits. We've done "Socks for Shelters" drives to help clothe the unhoused. Next, we're doing a big event for Meals on Wheels. We try to help in any way possible, and it's very rewarding and fulfilling.

While we learned a lot in the first six months, we continue to learn a tremendous amount. We always learn something new from David and the Trusted Advisors because the deeper you get in with them, the more you understand the complexity of the investments and the more you want to understand how things work. We may not be newbies anymore, but the learning never stops. We love the camaraderie. The world is ever-changing, so there's always something new and fascinating to learn.

Now, we're very comfortable where we are in Freedom Founders and in life. We are in a place where we can even give advice and mentorship to the new folks. Recently we brought three of our friends to a meeting. When you're experiencing freedom and all its tangible benefits, it's something you want to share.

We all have the same struggles and worries as people and couples and practice owners, so we love helping out newbies—especially the younger ones. We're almost jealous! We think, *Can you imagine if someone had talked to us about what is possible when we were that age?* But whether they're young or old, seeing the excitement of new folks has become one of the most rewarding aspects of our life. Freedom can make possible the impossible. What's better than that?

GETTING THE BAND BACK TOGETHER
DAVID'S TAKEAWAYS:

For James and Sara, like so many, hard work and the ability to generate income through the business were a given. But the uncertainty of not having a viable plan that would allow them to enjoy the fruits of their labor sooner, not later, was troubling. They saw their light at the end of the tunnel when they realized they had found their tribe—the Freedom Founders community. A place where the people are collaborative—not competitive.

Getting the band back together means James and Sara can enjoy much more time with family and friends, including their son, Zachary, and their new daughter-in-law, Brooke.

CHAPTER 3

DR. ANDY AND SUSANNE BABER

Mid-career, after playing it safe in investing, I started to think: *Why not get into some alternative investments?*

At the time, I was nine years into private practice as an oral surgeon in Arkansas, and things were going well. I had a young family and my wife, Susanne, and I had started dating when we were in high school, so we had spent the last decade-plus going through dental school, residency, and then getting the practice established. All in all, things were good, but I had a nagging sense that I wasn't going to want to practice indefinitely, and certainly not at the pace that I had been going. So why not dabble in real estate?

I started by consuming content online and listening to podcasts about various ways to get into real estate. Then I started having conversations with my friend group, where I got introduced to a friend of a friend who was building some spec houses with a local builder. There were some lots for sale in town close by us, and we were intrigued by the idea that we could buy the lots, the builder could build the house, and then we could split the profits from the eventual home sale.

Fortunately, it didn't turn out to be a disaster, but it definitely didn't go as planned. There was so much I didn't understand about the construction world, and how ground-up construction is just a riskier investment model in general—especially when the parties involved in the deal are inexperienced.

Of course, we invested in not one but two of these projects, which were supposed to take six months but ended up taking a year and went over budget. I got out by the skin of my teeth, after taking a very small loss, and realized, "Oh my goodness, I have no business playing in this space." If it hadn't been for the help of some great people that I got to know along the way—in particular, a guy at the title company who had a whole career's worth of experience in development and a realtor friend who sold the houses for me for a very modest fee—it would've been really painful. But it ended up being a good learning experience. In fact, it might have been just the right thing to happen to me, because I was able to very quickly grasp that I was playing in an arena that was outside of my expertise.

After having that experience, I still believed that investing in real estate made sense, but I understood implicitly that I needed help doing it and that going it alone was probably a good way to set me

> *I still believed that investing in real estate made sense, but I understood implicitly that I needed help doing it and that going it alone was probably a good way to set me up for failure.*

up for failure. And I had some sense of urgency; with our young family, I could see a day coming when I would want to have more flexibility and time to create meaningful experiences with my kids and my wife, and to be more present for them.

For most of my working life, I had a sense in the back of my mind that the traditional financial model—saving throughout your whole career, hoping at the end you have enough money to retire on, then perpetually siphoning off a little bit of that nest egg while hoping you don't run out of money before you die—wasn't the smartest approach. I was surrounded by friends and family who were well entrenched in this conventional paradigm, but I was slowly figuring out that I needed to look for an alternative. I almost intuitively knew that cash flow and replacement income were going to be the ticket, but initially, I didn't know how to articulate it or execute it.

Through the magic of the internet and Facebook, after reading and subscribing to a host of financial freedom podcasts and websites, I found David Phelps and Freedom Founders. I started watching the content and became interested, and that's really all it took. I just called and signed up for a call. The rest is history.

Before becoming a member, I went to my first event in 2017. My wife and I approached the event with a bit of skepticism. We understood that there was going to be a cost to participate in Freedom Founders and that the cost might be substantial. You don't want to spend a bunch of money on something that's not going to have a real tangible return on investment. So I think prospective members, even today, who come to a Freedom Founders event are justifiably skeptical.

But like the others, we got comfortable quickly and realized this wasn't pie in the sky. It wasn't too good to be true. It was the real deal.

We saw in the community of people at the event that the social proof was there. Numerous Freedom Founders members took us under their wing during and after the event. Many were just normal practicing dentists like we were, but there was social proof everywhere that this was a worthwhile endeavor. We got comfortable and joined right away.

Spousal Support and Participation Was Critical

Having Susanne at the first event was critical. Freedom Founders understand this better than anybody, the value of couples participating together. I'd recommend to someone, "Don't come to an event unless your spouse can come with you!" Because at the end of the day, you can't fully appreciate the life-changing effect of this organization if you're not in the room. It goes so much further than just David himself or the team or the Trusted Advisors. It's the members and the whole collective.

What happens after the meeting I best describe as positive peer pressure. You have goals, and the community helps you strive to meet them. These goals start off as financial but quickly morph into being about so much more, such as quality time, significance, health, and legacy. These goals become more tangible when you start heading in the right direction.

No member started out with freedom. They all put in the work, took the time, and learned everything they needed to. Some are a little further down the road than others, but those ahead are showing the way to those catching up. That sort of camaraderie is unique, especially in professional organizations, which are usually competitive. I also met a bunch of interesting people and immediately started making friendships that are now a very important part of my life five years later.

I joined Freedom Founders when I was 39, so I got an early start compared to most. I remember thinking, *"Oh, man, this would have been so great if I'd been here five years ago! You know, how much further ahead I would've been?"* But, with the benefit of hindsight, the nice thing I've realized is that it doesn't matter when you join. It just matters that you're here now. As long as you work the program, you're going to be fine. The investments will work in any market. You have to be diligent, put your nose down, and do the work, but you can get there.

Susanne and I walked away from the first meeting knowing we had found our Plan B. For me, that meant I was going to commit, hardcore. By that I mean I was very interested in the nuts and bolts of real estate investing. The details may not be of interest to everyone, but once I peeked behind the curtain and got a sense of how it worked, I was hooked. The Trusted Advisors, who are vetted and extremely capable; the different vehicles of investment; turnkey property lending; I could go on. There's just so much that I had never even heard of that was fascinating to me.

My creativity was stimulated like it hadn't been in years. After you've been in dental practice for a while, there are ways to keep yourself interested as far as expanding your clinical skills and business skills, but once you get things dialed in, work becomes pretty routine. I'd hit that point in my career where the day-to-day grind of the job just wasn't that exciting, so this was a whole different avenue to explore that really tickled my creative urges. But the creative side was even better because it was tangible work toward financial freedom so that I can have more time and create the life that I want for my family.

I spent the next four-plus years soaking up everything like a sponge. I completed all the training, calls, and educational modules to get up to speed as rapidly as I could.

Even today, the passion to learn and be creative hasn't dimmed. There's always the next level that you can go to, to learn and expand your knowledge base and experience.

In the beginning, the biggest thing I learned was to shift my mindset. Sure, there are all sorts of specific tactics and strategies that you implement in investing, but at a higher level, Freedom Founders is about changing how you think about life and money. It's about shifting your mindset from paper assets to tangible assets; from accumulation to cash flow. There are a gazillion different ways to do that, so the big picture shift is the most important part of it.

Freedom is constantly changing depending on where you're at in the process, but very early on, I just knew that I was trading time for dollars. I wanted to be able to do that less, but I didn't want to have to accept a lot of compromise in terms of lifestyle. Not that our lifestyle is anything extravagant, but I had a certain level of income that met the lifestyle needs that I had. That income required an input of time and energy that over the long run, I felt was not going to be sustainable.

That's where freedom started for me—the ability to buy some of my time back. And that's really where I still am. As a 43-year-old, my intention in the short term is not to stop practicing surgery altogether. Freedom is an incremental process for me. Right now, it looks like working four days a week instead of five. It looks like taking more time off to spend with my family on vacation. It looks like taking an extra week off to go to Peru to participate in a surgical mission trip. It looks like increasing my presence with the people that I care about. It looks like having the bandwidth and resources to take my extended family on that trip to Mexico that we did last year. It looks like creating those meaningful memories.

The added layer of financial freedom has empowered my ability to do those things and deliver those things. That's what freedom's looking like for me right now, even though what I describe is only a step along the way. It's not the full manifestation of what it will be, but it's a good place to start.

Freedom, if I could summarize it in a sentence, is being able to go with my family on spring break. That may not seem like a big deal, but for me, it's huge.

You see, as an oral surgeon, I remove a lot of wisdom teeth, most frequently in teenagers and young adults. Our busy times correspond to when there are breaks in the school year, such as summer or winter break. For whatever reason, spring break is our busiest week of the year. It's historically the most profitable week in our specialty suite, so I'd never been willing to take that week off. It certainly wasn't a big deal when my kids were itty bitty, but then they grew up, and for some reason, I still felt I had to work over spring break.

My Mindset Was Holding Me Back

It was all mental. I had a mental resistance to allowing myself the freedom to take that week off. I knew that the economic hit I was going to take wasn't significant in terms of paying the bills, but I hated to give up such a juicy week.

A while back, my wife, my kids, and I had started getting involved in a group trip to Colorado to go snow skiing on spring break with a bunch of our local friends and neighbors. It was a super fun community trip to Colorado. The first year that happened, I didn't go at all. Susanne and our son went and I stayed home with our youngest kid and worked. I didn't think much about it at the time.

The following year, I decided to take the first weekend of spring break to attend a specialty training course in Houston. I went to the airport with my wife and kids, who were there to fly to Colorado for the annual ski trip. After they boarded their flight, I went and sat at my gate. As I sat there, I had this sick-to-my-stomach feeling. I thought, *"I can't believe my wife and kids are on their way to spend a week in Colorado without me. I can't believe I've allowed this to happen. How stupid am I?"* I felt nauseous.

I had voluntarily given up a week with my family that I could never get back. It was a true "aha" moment.

In subsequent years, I started going on the trip, but only for three days. It took a couple more years after the "aha" moment for me to take the whole dang week off. Finally, I could say, *"If I miss out on a wisdom tooth bonanza, that'll just be okay."* It's not worth missing out on the limited number of experiences that will happen in my kid's childhood.

My son, Kelso, is 12, and I got to thinking that I really only have four or five more of these spring break weeks before it's gone. He'll go off to college and move on with the next part of his life. He's going to have his own stuff going on. The chance to ski with my kids at this age is a one-and-done opportunity.

As I built my passive income and my financial freedom started becoming more tangible and real, it helped shift my mindset to see that I didn't need to work over spring break. What I would've made during spring break, I can make up for in passive income. Now, two years and counting, I've gone for the full spring break family trip, never missing a day. I've seen my kids progress from griping about going to ski school to skiing black diamonds and moguls. With these knees, I can't keep up!

When you have more freedom in your life, you can do things that you put off for years. You can kind of return to that youthful mindset where the world is full of possibilities and there are opportunities around every corner; where you can chase your passions and hobbies and not have to put them on the back burner.

Beyond the financial impact of Freedom Founders, my involvement with the group has become much bigger, in particular regarding health and fitness.

When I first joined, I was somewhat on the journey to

> **When you have more freedom in your life, you can do things that you put off for years.**

getting healthier. I had achieved a bit of weight loss, but fitness wasn't a huge part of my life. It wasn't until some guys in our group started creating positive peer pressure that I took my health to the next level. The big change happened when my good friend Marck de Lautour, a Trusted Advisor, pushed me about what I was doing for exercise.

"Not a whole lot," was my response.

"You need a coach," he said. "As a high performer, you have a coach in your financial life. You obviously understand the concept that good coaching is worth paying for because it helps you produce the results that you want. So you need to hire a trainer or a fitness coach to improve your fitness." At the same time, another Trusted Advisor in our group, Mark Jackson, had started doing triathlons and had even become an Ironman. He's in his fifties, so that was extremely inspirational to see. He just decided fitness was important and he did it until he performed at a high level.

Through my network, I met and became friends with a guy who is a triathlon coach and multi-Ironman world-class athlete in his own right, Jason Wilford. I had just run a 5k, so I was taking baby steps in the right direction. Jason came into my life in May and said, "Let me train you up. Let's do a sprint triathlon on Labor Day weekend. You've got four months to prepare. I can get you there."

Before I knew it, he had me training hard. On top of that, over the course of our training, *without* him telling me, he bumped up my training schedule to Olympic distance.

Six weeks out from race day, he says, "Oh, by the way, I signed you up for the Olympic triathlon. I didn't tell you, but you've been training for the Olympic distance this whole time. You're right on schedule and ready for it!"

By that point, I had started to get in better shape, and I had much more confidence. I did the Olympic trials. Fast forward to May of last year, and I did a 70.3 half Ironman race. Health, fitness, Ironman—that all came from Freedom Founders. Having a peer group that recognizes that freedom in life has to be more than financial because it doesn't mean a lot without your health has been a tangible improvement in my life.

Being around the right people now, having the tension between where you are and where you want to be in your mind, and then understanding the value of not going it alone can help you go far. Dentistry is very much a solo activity for so many of us. I have partners now, but for a long time, I was by myself. We get insulated in our little office cocoons. We don't think collaboratively, because that's not how dentistry works. But it is how freedom works.

Freedom Founders, above all, changes your mindset. You realize a lot of things work so much better, and the results are so much more fruitful if it's collaborative and there's a team involved. That's certainly true of the fitness journey that I have taken because I would never have been able to hold myself to the discipline and training that it took to condition myself to go do a half Ironman.

When there's a community of other people that are holding me accountable towards achieving my goal, everything's possible. I've got a coach, a community, a goal, and a deadline, so all I need to do is race. I'm going to be embarrassed if I don't put the effort

DR. ANDY AND SUSANNE BABER

into conditioning myself, so I train. That's the model I used for fitness, but it all came from Freedom Founders. Coach, community, goal, effort—that culture is what makes Freedom Founders such a refreshing place to be for new and veteran members alike. It's been such an unexpected joy to be a part of this group.

Susanne's Insight & Observation

A huge turning point for us occurred when Andy committed to creating the Freedom to not miss another family trip or spring break with us. We only have so many more chances to create experiences together as a family before the kids are grown and gone.

I want our kids to understand that you can work hard, but your whole life doesn't have to be about work. You need to find balance in having time that you spend with friends and family. You can't put a price on Freedom of time.

I'm so proud of Andy for making the commitment to be present with us as a family.

GETTING THE BAND BACK TOGETHER
DAVID'S TAKEAWAYS:

Dr. Andy Baber has a curiosity that makes him not only inquisitive but also forces him to challenge the status quo. As a successful oral surgeon in a multi-doctor practice, Andy felt the pressure that his success has created: NO TIME!

For Andy Baber, getting the band back together meant no longer leaving his family on spring break to do work "because that's what oral surgeons do during spring break." Having a Freedom Blueprint Plan that he and Susanne could measure with certainty gave Andy the freedom to make the very significant decision to "buy his time back" without guilt.

Additionally, Dr. Baber found that "Do-It-Yourself" investing without real expertise, competence, or experience entailed too much risk (and stress). Freedom Founders was the community that he longed for; a network and friendships that would allow him to continue his alternative investing path but without the unknowns and potential losses in both money and time.

"Justified skepticism" of what Freedom Founders was all about is a common theme for the majority of those on the outside looking in. "This has to be too good to be true. There must be a catch here somewhere" are often spoken words from guests who attend their first Freedom Founders meeting. And, as is usually the case, it was Susanne, the intuitive spouse, who read the culture and values of the membership and who became the advocate for the freedom that both she and Andy wanted for their family.

CHAPTER 4

DR. DENNIS AND MONZELL PERRY

Sometimes it's hard to believe where our lives have ended up. When I was breaking my back over a dental chair back in the '90s, I certainly wouldn't have believed that I would be living my best life thirty years later. I had thought about retirement but had no idea how to build wealth. Now, we own two very nice homes—one in Cincinnati, and the other at the foothills of the Smoky Mountains on a lake called Calico in East Tennessee. While my wife, Monzell, and I have never been big travelers, when something comes up that we want to do, we go without worrying about the cost. That means we get to spend as much time with our grandchildren as we please. I spend the rest of my free time practicing my cooking and learning to play guitar. I might not be *very* good but it's fun and meaningful to me. What's truly liberating about our lives is that we don't spend time worrying about money.

I used to think I would have to spend my golden years hunched over a dental chair or hoping whatever pile of money I managed to amass would last until we died. Even after I had sold my practice and invested in the stock market, financial

> *What's truly liberating about our lives is that we don't spend time worrying about money.*

planners told me the best I could hope for was stretching that pile of money until we were about 92. Now we are hoping to live into our hundreds and leave an inheritance, and we truly owe it all to Freedom Founders.

I was an oral and maxillofacial surgeon by trade. I went into practice with an older gentleman in 1988. Two years later, I bought the practice and went solo. I remained a solo practitioner for about five years before bringing my partner in. It was a hospital-based practice, which is pretty rare in the oral surgery world. I worked in the hospital, so there was constantly something to do between hospital patients and the E.R. It was very demanding; we rarely took time off. I was on call 24-7 and at work six days a week. It was grueling and it wasn't getting any easier with age.

I started to feel burnt out. I didn't want to keep doing this for the rest of my life, but I didn't know how else to make money. So, I started learning about the stock market. I figured that I'm a reasonably intelligent guy, so I should be able to figure this out. I spent a bunch of money on programs and thought I had a handle on things. Unfortunately, I made some bad investments.

A friend of mine was an options trader out of Lexington, Kentucky. He taught me a strategy using the 30-year bond futures market. I was doing credit spreads, where I would buy a call or a put option, then sell one a little bit closer to the money. That gave me some backside protection. For example, if I thought the bond market was going up, I would see a put and then buy a put just a little bit further out of the money to protect me in case I was wrong. I did that over and over again. There was a formula you could employ, so if I wanted a 97% probability of success, it would tell me what strike prices I should be on the lookout for to have that rate of success. If you look at the risk/reward, it was a terrible trade; my risk was probably $1,000 and my profit was $150, but the probability of success was so high that you could just do it over and over again. So, after having some success with it, I started to get cocky. I'm a bright guy, I thought. I know what I'm doing.

Feeling very sure of myself, I started doing some naked options, meaning I didn't have the protection on the downside. I stopped playing it safe and figured, I had been right so many times, and with a naked option, I'd be able to keep more money. I got brazen and had 30 naked puts. At that point, I was up many thousands of dollars. That's when the market corrected eight points in a single night. That is a huge correction for the futures market. In twenty-four hours, I went from being way up to several thousand dollars in the hole. I got a margin call from the brokerage telling me I was negative and needed to send them money that day. You hear stories about how the market crashes and people jump off buildings—well, let me just say that I get it!

I Lost All of Our Money

I had to call Monzell and ask her to come into the office because I needed to speak with her. She thought someone must've died or some kind of tragedy had happened at work. "I lost all our money," I told her, utterly defeated and sure she was going to want to kill me.

"What are you talking about?" she asked. I told her about what had happened in the trade and how I had lost everything we'd saved. I expected her to yell or even slap me—she would have had the right. Instead, she reassured me. "It's only money. We'll be okay. We'll save it up again." How many spouses would have done that? She is truly remarkable.

After that, I had done a lot more reading on building wealth, and I realized that every wealthy person seemed to have real estate in their portfolio. We found this investment group around 2005 and joined, despite some red flags. The head of this group was so eager to recruit dentists that she made me a coach with zero experience. Then we started trying to accumulate a portfolio of houses to rent out. We bought seven or eight homes all together between October and December of 2007, which as you probably know, was not great timing. We were managing six of those properties, and I was trying to do everything on my own. It wasn't making my life any easier; in fact, it was a second job that made me quite miserable.

I was spending more time working than ever before and less and less time with my family. My day job was killing my neck and back, too. I had just undergone my fourth back surgery, so I was counting on these investments. Unfortunately, the market crashed and scuttled those plans. We had used our home equity credit line for those down payments, and we came really close to having the loan called from our bank. Luckily, they were a private bank and gave me some leeway when I begged. I had to, embarrassingly, borrow money from a friend to pay down the loan. We were able to get out of those properties without losing money, but we certainly didn't make any money, either.

I was beginning to think I was cursed with bad timing. Maybe retiring wealthy just wasn't in the cards for me. Perhaps all I could hope for was enough money that I could afford to stop working.

My back was killing me, and I had a contract in place that said I needed to give two years' notice before I retired. So, in 2017, I made that decision and gave my notice that I would retire at the close of 2019.

At this point, all of our money was in the stock market and being managed by financial planners. We had annuities and a pretty traditional portfolio. We had a few different people look at everything, and they all told us that as long as the stock market behaved for the first two or three years after my retirement, we should be fine. The projections showed that the money we had should have lasted until we were 92 years old, which we figured was fine, as no one in either of our families had lived that long, and we would still have a little bit left. Nobody could predict how much, but they said that based on a very conservative 6 percent growth rate, we would be fine.

Well, the first thing we noticed is that even when the market was very strong, we were only seeing about 4–4.5 percent growth after everyone took their fees. So, we were already concerned that those projections were not going to hold. That was December 31, 2019, just three months before COVID shut down the world and the bottom completely dropped out of the stock market. My terrible timing had struck again. Now, the market came back fairly quickly, but at the time, we had no way of knowing that or how bad it was going to get. I had visions of myself hunched over a chair at 75 years old, pulling teeth again. It was a very stressful time.

I Was Tired of the Wall Street Roller Coaster

I don't recall exactly how David Phelps and I first crossed paths. He is active in our market, so I was probably aware of him before first hearing him on a podcast. I do remember that I really liked what he had to say. He seemed sharp and knowledgeable, but I was resistant to any sort of in-person meetings or groups after our previous experiences. In retrospect, I wish we had taken the opportunity sooner, but with everything we had been through, I was pretty cynical about joining anything or putting any money into new ventures. My wife had begged me not to join that other investment group, and I hadn't listened to her. I had a lot of guilt and remorse about that and was not about to make the same mistake. However, David's people reached out to me again a few months later and invited me to attend a virtual meeting as a guest. I was intrigued, but there was no way I was going to so much as attend an online event without running it by my wife.

At this point, I hadn't so much as mentioned David or Freedom Founders to Monzell. We had just managed to finally sell our last rental house in 2018, and I had sworn I was never going to get involved with real estate ever again. So, I talked with Monzell, and told her about this guy, David Phelps, who was a dentist and a real estate investor. I told her I had had a few calls with him and listened to some podcasts, and I thought he had some interesting ideas. We both agreed that there was no harm in attending the virtual meeting since we wouldn't have to travel or put any real money into it. We agreed that we would listen and if we started feeling like it was similar to the trap we had fallen into before, we would just graciously turn off the computer and that would be the end of it.

David's Sincerity and Humbleness Overwhelmed Us

That first night, the thing that really stood out to us was David's sincerity. This was a man who had accomplished so much but was still so humble and gracious. We could tell that he genuinely cared for the community, its members, and its guests. At one point he said, "Frankly, I don't particularly care if you join this organization or not," so there was no pressure being exerted on us as we'd experienced with that other organization.

The night ended, and Monzell and I looked at each other and agreed we would like to see what was going on the next day. So, we tuned in again and listened to a lot of stuff about dental practices. There was a lot of anxiety over COVID and what was going to happen to people's practices. It impressed me how the sessions were geared towards focusing on what was current and the concerns people were dealing with at the time.

The community itself was full of knowledgeable people, all coming together to support one another. I was sold. I really thought it was a good move for us, but I was not going to lead us there. Monzell needed to be on board with this, too. I was thinking, *"God, I hope she likes this."* Then she looked at me and said, "You know what? I think we need to join this." They even offered us a discount because of the pandemic. Everything seemed to fall into place. I had just been paid out for my practice, so we had a nice chunk of money sitting in the bank that we were trying to figure out what to do with. We had financial planners with all sorts of ideas about how to put it to work in the market, but we didn't feel that was the right decision. By the next day, we'd committed, and ever since, it has been such a wild ride.

We were a bit unique, as far as Freedom Founders members go. Most people who join are relatively young—they've got five to ten years left to work, and a lot of them own their own buildings and practices when they come into the organization. All that was already behind me, which is one of the reasons I think it was so easy for us to reach Free for Life™ status. We already knew what our lifestyle burn rate was and we were already living it. All we had to do was secure assets that would generate that amount of money, or as close as we could get. We didn't start with a huge pool of money, either, because I had blown so much of it on bad investments. Nonetheless, Freedom Founders worked for us and it has been amazing.

When David talks about living in freedom, it is God's honest truth. That's what it really comes down to at the end of the day: do you want to be able to give yourself the freedom to live your best life, or do you want to be stuck, working your life away and never having the time or the money to do the things that truly matter to you? Thanks to Freedom Founders, I have the freedom to spend more time with my family, pursue hobbies that bring me joy, and enjoy a comfortable lifestyle. We have two gorgeous homes and plenty of time to share with those we love.

We used to think living to 92 would be good, if we could afford it. But now, we want to live until at least our 75th anniversary. So we want to hold on until at least 102. And the way our assets generate money, we could afford to live until 192 if we had to—though granted, I'm not sure I'd want to live that long, even if science enabled it. But if we had to, we could afford to. Once we do depart this plane of existence, there will be a nice nest egg for our children and grandchildren. That's a legacy I never thought I would have, and one that I hope will help my children and their children's children to live free as well.

GETTING THE BAND BACK TOGETHER
DAVID'S TAKEAWAYS:

For Dennis and Monzell Perry, getting the band back together came from the realization that with a measured financial plan not tied to the volatile stock market, they could keep both of their primary homes, travel, and spend time with their family without wondering if they "had enough" to sustain the rest of their life post-retirement.

As is common for business owners and entrepreneurs used to doing everything themselves, Dennis had tried his hand at options trading and real estate investment on his own. Both strategies failed.

Freedom Founders was admittedly a stretch, especially considering Monzell wasn't a fan of their participation in the prior real estate group, but after vetting the group as only a woman with a sixth sense can do, Monzell was fully on board.

Today, Dr. and Mrs. Perry are Free for Life™ members and part of the Frontier group within the Freedom Founders community.

CHAPTER 5

DR. JIM AND CINDA RACHOR

I grew up the son of a financial advisor who was a Wall Street employee for fifty years. He did quite well, but I saw that he was never really happy. In fact, he was quite lonely. I also grew up not knowing a lot about finances. I just knew that you're supposed to work hard for forty years, give your money to somebody to invest for you, and hope it's enough until the end. But nobody ever knows what that number is. How much is enough?

In my career, I was a fairly successful dentist, making a very good income. The trouble was, I didn't have any money unless I was working, so I was trading time for dollars. Being wealthy on paper, but having to work all the time, meant I wasn't happy and didn't have any free time. At some point, I realized that I was probably doing it wrong. I also realized I didn't know anything about investing. That seemed to be backward from what I should be doing.

As a semi-intelligent person, *could I learn a little bit of the financial acumen to find a better way to invest?*

> *As a semi-intelligent person, could I learn a little bit of the financial acumen to find a better way to invest?*

Freedom Founders provided the approach I needed with alternative investments out of the stock market. Now I have one degree of separation from the people I invest with. The person I invest money with is not just a manager, but a decision-maker in exactly where that money goes. I can go visit them to learn directly about the product and service provided, unlike the stock market where you never know exactly where your money goes. The best part is these alternative investments provide cash flow, so I could make money while I was sleeping.

Passive Income Strategies Were Never Taught

This approach—which really starts with a mindset of passive income over active income—wasn't taught to me or anybody who is a dentist, doctor, lawyer, or other practice professional.

It all started when I threw my back out by working too much. This is common for dentists. There I was, laying down in bed for the week, and I just couldn't move. So I read. I read *The Art of the Deal*, by Donald Trump. I read *Rich Dad, Poor Dad*, by Robert T. Kiyosaki and Sharon Lechter, and I read *From High Income to High Net Worth*, by David Phelps. A friend of mine who had invested with my father had recommended the title, and when I read David's book, it resonated.

As soon as I opened the book's first page, I started to wonder, *Why didn't anybody ever tell me about this approach to money?* In bed with my back thrown out, I was unhappy and extremely motivated to create a business where I could do other things while making a passive income.

Everything I read corroborated what I'd read about in David's book, so I contacted him and signed up to attend an event. My wife didn't go to the first event; she thought it was a cult of some sort! Plus, we were "happily" invested with my dad and didn't think much about our money or our life beyond our working years.

At my first meeting, I talked to the members and the Trusted Advisors, and while everything checked out, I was diligent. After the meeting, I visited each TA one-on-one where they worked. I traveled around the country to their businesses, and I learned then what I believe wholeheartedly now—David Phelps is the best vetter of people that I've ever met.

When I came home after the meeting, I told my wife about it. She didn't believe it was as great as I said. It's hard to convey to someone if they weren't there.

Over the next month, I bought ten properties, because I was hooked. Over the next five years, from that first one until today, I've missed only one meeting, and everything I heard about in the first meeting has come true beyond my expectations.

Before Freedom Founders, all I owned was my office building and my home. The rest of it, my dad managed. What I've since learned is that if you're in the market, you're only in one asset class. You're not as diversified as people think. Stocks and bonds are just part of one asset class that's subject to major crashes.

It's funny, but everybody I thought was so "financially smart" was working forty hours a week. It didn't make sense to me. The people managing my money weren't free for life, so why am I giving them all my money if they're not living how I aspire to live?

I've never met anybody who has gone back to Wall Street from real estate. I must say that the Freedom Founders approach is different from most real estate investing, where people try to buy a rental on their own, try to learn about it on their own, and then try to manage it on their own. David created a vehicle where it's passive; you don't have to do it on your own. Instead, you can invest in it, learn about it to whatever degree you wish, and enjoy the cash flow.

For me, I love the Freedom Founders approach. I also love the other aspects, like lending and the various deals, but what I love the most is that I'm free. My passive income is now more than my dental income ever was, and I had a very large practice of over 5,000 patients, which I sold six months ago. I was doing great—as long as I was there in the office—but I'm doing even better now.

Freedom Allowed Me to Focus on 'My Next'

Today I have an organization called the Smile Mentorship Institute, which involves me going into dental schools and preaching what David's talking about. There I promote David's books and teach dental students about the business side of the industry and the investment side of dentistry. I do this for free because I'm passionate about educating young students and grads. Plus, they don't have any money anyway!

My main concern right now is the young professionals out there. I see two major problems. First, students graduate school with a ton of debt. Second, they are cornered into prioritizing dollars over service.

Graduates don't typically own their own practice but rather become a W-2 earner in someone else's practice, which means they don't have a lot of ways to mitigate taxes. Thus, their treatment plans are a bit heavy because they need to pay back all their loans. On top of that, every dental practice, unfortunately, is valued by how much money it makes, not by the quality of service. These are major problems for every young dentist who's doing this, following the herd, and trying to work as long as they can, as much as they can, to catch up to the debt.

During my visits to the dental school classrooms, the first thing I say when I walk in the room is, "Hey, real quick. What was your favorite business class in dental school?"

The response is always crickets. They get real quiet and listen. Because they know they're going to get out of school and just follow the herd. They buy life insurance and malpractice insurance. They buy a house. Then they go work for somebody and pay their bills after their taxes as a W-2 income earner. They're behind the eight-ball compared to the generation of dentists who own a practice, own a building, and have no student debt. The situation isn't good.

Now I only work a couple of days a week, but I'm the best kind of dentist. I don't need the money, I like what I do, and I'm not stressed out like everybody else. Every other dentist I know who's not Free for Life™ is not practicing stress-free. I'll talk to these older practicing dentists, and it's almost like they're in prison. They'll say, "Oh, man, I've been in 30 years" or "I've got 22 years." It's sad.

I was that person. I was working too hard, depressed, and watching my family go on vacation while I was working. When your hands dictate your income every day, you are not free, and that's what's happening to most dentists.

I have seven kids. We adopted two girls from Guatemala. My wife and I do a lot of mission work around the world, mostly with orphans in Guatemala. Now I have the free time to do what my "next" is. David's book, *What's Your Next?* really opened my eyes to thinking about my freedom and retirement years in a new light.

For me, my "next" is setting up our legacy for the next generation. I'm in the midst of building a family office, which will contribute to my children's financial legacy but also ensure a legacy of helping others, especially orphans.

My kids, my wife, and I formed a family office. This is a large family office that does investing as a team. I learned about family offices from studying the Rockefeller and Rothschild families. It takes some doing, because you have to look at yourself and finances as part of a team, and it takes a teamwork structure, but it has so many expected and unexpected benefits. The best part is that it's helped my kids learn about investing. They know all about alternative investments, lending deals, joint ventures, arbitrage, and related documentation. They each have their own LLC and an irrevocable trust. They own turnkey lending deals in their own right and they can create a home office and deduct some expenses at their homes. They're way ahead of almost everybody out there, and it was essential to me they had this type of education early in life.

We're also building a family bank, likewise copying that from the Rockefellers. It has an infinite banking structure where we have parameters, allowing it to function as the mothership that creates the cash flow.

Rather than just hand my kids a chunk of money, we're having them partake in a portion of this business that creates cash flow. I believe that you don't just want to give kids a big bag of money—you want to teach them. The old adage is, "Don't hide the dynamite," which means you don't want them to suddenly inherit millions with no training on how to use it. To me, that's akin to abuse!

As I tell my kids, I don't love money. I don't love it at all, but I use it. I use it for doing things that are good. I'm a proponent of not being rich, but being a wealthy person. A wealthy person has a mindset that is "other" oriented. We teach our kids to be significant rather than successful. We're big on helping them create their own passions and legacy. These topics are so important to me that I wrote a book about them!

This approach also involves taking our kids to Guatemala and working in environments with those who are less fortunate and seeing kids their age who are struggling. It involves creating a "family boardroom" where, once a quarter, you get together with no phones and have a family meeting. You tell your kids how important your wife is to you. You tell them how important the family name is. It involves living by the four agreements: Tell the truth; Do your best; Don't take things personally; Don't assume things.

David and Freedom Founders gave me the financial model for opening the door to freedom. Once you open that door, there is a world of possibilities.

Other than your family, time is your greatest asset, and David allows us to get that back. When you're constantly pursuing time, it's chasing you as well. That's what many forget. They spend all their lives in these little buildings hunched over big chairs, not realizing that they're giving up their whole life. For what?

GETTING THE BAND BACK TOGETHER
DAVID'S TAKEAWAYS:

For Dr. Jim Rachor, getting the band back together involved his family (seven children, of whom two are adopted), the next generation of young students, and their family involvement with mission work in Guatemala. TIME without stress or compression is what Jim finds to be so freeing and he desperately wants to pass on this message to all who would hear it.

Like many Freedom Founders members, Jim is a voracious reader. He was always searching for another way to create the wealth that would ultimately give him the freedom and choice that he craved in life. Freedom Founders became a community that would allow him to take his passion for learning and apply it to a proven model where he's only "one degree of separation" from his money (unlike Wall Street, where there are numerous disconnects between the investor and their money).

Becoming a Free for Life™ member has allowed Jim to have ultimate freedom in his life. He is no longer handcuffed to a trading-time-for-dollars mindset and has created an investment portfolio that provides the cash flow that supports his family's lifestyle. Taking charge of your own financial future is a key construct in the Freedom Founders community.

CHAPTER 6

DR. DORA LEE

It was time to step up my financial game. Mid-career, I had been in practice for about fifteen years and had saved up some cash to invest. I knew this would be the engine to get me to retirement sooner. I had a sense of investing and grew up with entrepreneurial parents. Their philosophy was to pay your debt, buy properties, and keep them in cash. Living in California, I felt some trepidation about putting a lot of money into real estate, as it's so expensive here.

Still, I got a rental home and a tenant—but it never was a real source of cash flow. I did it for the appreciation. Meanwhile, I was barely breaking even.

Then I bought a piece of commercial property with a group of friends, one of whom was a real estate agent. We bought it in cash. Our strategy was to sit on it so that it would later become pure cash flow.

My friends and I didn't all agree on the idea of leverage, and buying it all in cash was probably not the smartest way to go about it. If I had known then what I know now because of Freedom Founders,

I would have done it differently. But it certainly wasn't worth losing friendships over, and it functions as debt-equity for me.

At the same time, I dabbled in the stock market. I tried to educate myself on it, but I never really understood it. Knowing there's a cyclical downturn every ten years or so just didn't sit right with me. How could you retire on something like that?

I Needed Guidance and Direction

Building my own dental practice had taken a lot of hard work, blood, sweat, and tears, but it paid off with a comfortable pool of savings. As I don't have kids, I never really had the accompanying financial burden like a lot of other people my age. How could I use this pool of money?

Also on my mind was travel. I had been bitten by the travel bug, and it had become more and more of a priority. Through it, I discovered a new passion: photography. The adventure of seeing the world and the creative fulfillment of photography gave me a taste of a life outside of work, and I wanted more of it.

Traveling also made me question my calling in life. I had gone back to school and gotten my Master of Public Health, thinking I could travel while using my dental background to help people internationally. Then COVID hit.

Luckily, I had stumbled upon Freedom Founders before the world turned upside down in March of 2020. I found the group on Facebook. My friend Audrey and I were in the same boat of having saved up enough, but not knowing the right strategies for achieving financial freedom. We didn't know it yet, but we needed a community and mentorship.

We couldn't find much online about Freedom Founders, so we went to investigate for ourselves. We attended our first meeting in San Diego with a healthy dose of skepticism. We immediately thought, "Why is everyone so happy?" All the speakers and members were so transparent and welcoming. We couldn't help but question, "Is this a cult? Where's the Kool-Aid?" But everyone was genuine. We were blown away by the supportive environment.

Once we committed to joining, we couldn't get enough; it was exciting to learn about, though at first, the lectures went over our heads. We realized there was a whole world of things that we couldn't learn on our own through books or even through friends. You really have to be in the community.

> "Why is everyone so happy?" All the speakers and members were so transparent and welcoming. We couldn't help but question, "Is this a cult? Where's the Kool-Aid?" But everyone was genuine.

As we got to know other members, we learned about their investments and deals. Every door we opened led to more learning, more connection, and more possibilities. We learned investment strategies that we never would have figured out on our own.

We learned that fast money is not necessarily the best and that you can't be distracted by shiny objects. We learned to look at the details and to ask the right questions. It's been nothing short of life-changing.

After networking with other Trusted Advisors (TAs) outside of California through Freedom Founders, I learned that real estate *in California* was not the best investment. So I did a 1031 exchange from one home and got four homes out of it, which tripled my cash flow. I was about to refi out of those, but the Freedom Founders network taught me the potential was so much greater than I realized. The network is not only members and friends but also Trusted Advisors, which made my investing strategies more sophisticated.

You get as much out of Freedom Founders as you put in. You can spend very little time, even an hour a week, and just focus on passive cash flow deals, or you can dig deep to truly understand your investments.

Audrey and I knew we wanted a growth strategy. That meant investing in commodities rather than just a fund. We wanted to set up an LLC. A growth approach made sense for where I am in my career; I still have a practice with a monthly income. I'm not as dependent on monthly cash flow as somebody who is retired and doesn't have that income stream coming in. I wanted to create savings that would grow later.

It was very helpful to join Freedom Founders with my friend because we had the same level of interest and commitment. I'm not married, and Audrey's husband wasn't involved in Freedom Founders, so learning all this together just made sense. Our place in life, goals, and paths were similar. We made it a point to talk weekly—almost daily— about deals.

Then, two more of our friends started to take notice. They witnessed the change in me as a result of Freedom Founders, and it made them want to join before even attending a meeting! Our group of four talks daily—our Freedom Founders chat has had about 30 texts back and forth just this morning!

Freedom Founders hasn't asked me to take on any sort of role in the group, but I feel compelled to mentor my friends who joined after me. I want to be a part of their journey and I can't wait for them to experience what I'm experiencing now. I get so energized when I go to meetings and talk to members; it's the highlight of my day. I'm always learning something new. It's been great to vet deals through other members and Trusted Advisors.

My decision to join in 2019 couldn't have been timed better. I had taken half my investments out of the stock market and put them in Freedom Founders, so when things went south in the stock market in March of 2020, I had checks coming in regularly from Freedom Founders. I wish I'd taken it all out of the stock market!

Before joining Freedom Founders, I thought of retirement as a countdown. *How many more years do I have to work? How many dollars do I need in the bank?*

Now, I know I have the money to pay for my expenses. I don't have to work if I don't want to, but because I'm able to cut back days without stressing about it, I enjoy my practice more. I now have two or three more decades that I can enjoy without worrying about a countdown. Freedom Founders has helped me pace myself. It's been a total paradigm shift.

I believe that surrounding yourself with smart people helps you to make smarter decisions. I realized that my accountant understood dentistry really well, but didn't speak the language of real estate. So after joining Freedom Founders, I switched accountants to someone who was in Freedom Founders, too.

Freedom Founders Has Been a Game-Changer

It's been a game-changer to have an accountant who not only helps me understand the tax implications of my decisions but who also deeply understands my goals and investments. I told him my goal was to work two clinical days instead of three, and that I want to take four to six weeks off for vacation per year.

In 2021, I did it. I visited Kenya and Iceland back to back. I was able to take six weeks off while my practice was still open and running. I enjoyed a genuine, rejuvenating break from it all—especially when I found myself in locations with no reception! I never would have been able to do that without Freedom Founders.

Because of COVID, and because of Freedom Founders, I realized that I can't put off the things in life I want to do. Going to Kenya and Iceland gave me mental clarity and physical freedom from the daily grind. My photography skills improved with all the practice I got during my trip, and I brought home some beautiful photographs. I felt so fortunate to have traveled internationally at a time when hardly anyone was able to.

When I made the decision to go away for six weeks, I was a bit nervous. I thought I might not get the chance again, so I took the leap. But after coming home, I realized that I can take six weeks off every year without hurting my practice.

I used to be too afraid to ask for more time off than two weeks per year. I always knew I wanted to do more than just be a dentist, but I didn't have the energy to pursue anything else. I didn't have the time to be curious.

One of the speakers at Freedom Founders said that "you can't go looking for your calling." I realized that to let my calling come to me, I needed to cultivate stillness—but how can I be still when I'm constantly working? *How can I give myself that time and space if I'm thinking about my overhead, staff, and patients?*

To be creative, you need time and space. I'm now able to give myself that. I can develop my photography skills, and I love that pursuing photography encourages me to travel. It brings out the other side of my brain: the creative side. When working, the brain is overstimulated by a million different things, but there is a meditative quality to photography: it makes you stop and observe the world around you. When photographing wildlife, you become part of the landscape. You see the beauty around you.

I love creating beauty and sharing it with others. It's my way of storytelling. Photography is how I share my travel experiences with others—the sounds, the smells, the bustle of street cars. I've started taking photography lessons to be able to do it at a higher level. It all comes from my initial love of traveling and learning about other cultures. It's very humbling to see how people live in countries other than your own.

When I first joined Freedom Founders, everyone kept saying, "I have clarity." I didn't know what that meant until now. When you're almost Free for Life™, you have clarity because you know how much you spend, how much you probably will spend, and how much is coming in. I'm not relying upon the unpredictability of the market or even my practice. Dental practices, like any business, deal with staff shortages, inflation, and the scariness of a looming recession.

Pre-Freedom Founders, I probably would have been more worried about my overhead, and pushing myself to work more in order to save more, but I don't have that fear anymore. I have financial clarity: I know the path to becoming Free for Life™. I'm not there yet, but I know I have the numbers to do it. I would love for my friends and myself to all become Free for Life™ at the same time.

Clarity on Financial Freedom Opens the Doors to Other Passions

Now that I have clarity on financial freedom, I'm on the path to freeing my other passions. The foundation of financial freedom allows me to invest in my travel and my photography, and to enjoy a life outside of work.

But paradoxically, I love the dental field now more than ever. So many dentists have burned out and sold their practice because of COVID, but it's just made it more clear to me how I want to structure my business to optimize my life.

Between COVID, family obligations, and the nature of the work, a lot of medical professionals are too busy to sit down and ask themselves the important, personal questions, like, "Why am I working so hard? What's the purpose?"

For me, legacy is a huge part of it. I'm in my 40s, and I'm still defining mine. I'm grateful that Freedom Founders gave me the time, space, support, and tools to do so. I'm in a better place to find my purpose in life than I have ever been before.

I'm on the path to becoming Free for Life™. I'll soon free myself up to pursue my ultimate dream, which is to do global nonprofit work. I've been to 25 countries and counting. Now that I know what I'm doing, in my work-life balance and in the field of photography, I'm planning to take another trip to Kenya! There are more animals to be photographed, more adventures to be had, and more good to do in the world.

GETTING THE BAND BACK TOGETHER
DAVID'S TAKEAWAYS:

Dr. Dora Lee is on the cusp of Free for Life™ status after less than three years as a Freedom Founders member. Though she came from an entrepreneurial culture, the methodology of real estate investment there was somewhat old school and geographically limited. After a few "Do-It-Yourself" attempts at building outside wealth and cash flow, Dora found that the community, network, and mindset shifts within Freedom Founders made up the approach that she needed.

Getting the band back together revolves around Dr. Lee's love for travel and photography. She is also purpose-driven to invest in global non-profit initiatives.

With her living expenses paid for by her asset-based (non-Wall Street) investments, she has given herself the permission to do more traveling, taking as much as six weeks off at a time. Having this margin of time allows Dora to focus more on her creative side which is where she blossoms.

The Freedom Founders community is the network that has opened the door to her "next" and a place to refer her friends and colleagues who also want what Dora Lee has.

CHAPTER 7

DR. AUDREY SHEU AND MARK WU

It never occurred to me that I could work less or retire early. My parents are immigrants with an incredible work ethic. They worked until they couldn't anymore, but between my kids and my practice, I felt like I never had enough time for anything. I wanted a way to dial back a little bit or have some supplemental income to take the load off myself. I wanted to do things that I wanted to do, rather than feeling pressured and obligated to do them.

All I knew from my childhood was to work hard. That's the immigrant mentality. My father worked six days a week, never wanted vacations, and then one day had a massive stroke. He was forced into retirement. He was expected to be bedridden for the rest of his life, but he ended up regaining some walking ability—though he could no longer drive and obviously couldn't work.

That was a wake-up call: you can't just keep working, working, working. You have got to enjoy life as you go along. I wanted some sort of income to feel safe doing that.

Fifteen years ago, I was diagnosed with lupus, an autoimmune disease. I haven't had any health issues arise because of this yet, but my friend with lupus, who is my age, has severe rheumatoid arthritis in her hands, ankles, and feet. Her hands are claw-like. If that ever flared up for me, I'd have to retire.

I didn't want to be completely dependent on my dentistry income. *What if my career ended one day because my disease went into high gear all of a sudden?*

I'm a pediatric dentist. After graduating from dental school in 2008, I got married and had kids right away, so life was hectic for a while.

My husband, Mark, an OB-GYN, is a total workaholic and was never home. I felt like a single mom at times. My kids are nine and five now, but back when they were both toddlers, I was barely keeping my head above water. I was anxious for them to be able to use the bathroom by themselves. I was so exhausted every day. I was ready to move on to the next phase of life.

My practice was stable, but I didn't do much to promote or grow it; I just let it flow. I was never struggling, but I didn't have a good grip on the state of my finances. I would just leave it to my Wells Fargo guy. As long as my statement wasn't negative, I was good. I didn't understand the stock market. I never really tracked how much I was making, saving, or spending. I knew I didn't spend that much, but I didn't know if I was truly saving up for retirement.

I Had a Lack of Knowledge but Was Willing to Learn

While I didn't really know what I was doing, I was aware of my lack of knowledge, so I started learning about my finances and potential ways to invest, including in real estate. I knew I couldn't manage rental properties when I barely had time to clean my own toilet! Plus, I had heard horror stories from my friends about rentals.

But around this time, my CPA introduced me to one of his clients who funds large real estate projects. I invested $25,000 into a syndication. My family told me it was a scam, but it came back in two years at a 33 percent return. That sparked my interest.

Then I saw David on Facebook. He spoke in a Facebook group for dentists who were moms. I saw that a Freedom Founders meeting was scheduled nearby in San Diego; *Why don't I just go?* I thought. I spoke with Dora Lee, my good friend, fellow dentist, and soon-to-be Freedom Founders member. *What do we have to lose?* We agreed: we'd drive down for the weekend, and if the folks there turned out to be crazy, then we'd just leave and have a nice week in San Diego!

We didn't know what to expect at the first meeting. In the age of too much information, it was bizarre that I couldn't find any specifics about Freedom Founders, aside from very positive feedback. I finally found a member who was willing to talk to me about it on the phone, but she was vague. She just told me how happy she was with it. She wasn't trying to be cryptic, but I wanted details. *Is the membership fee worth it? Did you earn it back in the first year?* Once you're in the group, you realize why these aren't the best questions.

But those in the mommy dental group and others I spoke to seemed genuine with their praise, so my interest was definitely piqued. I wanted to find out what it was all about for myself.

There are a lot of younger Freedom Founders members now, but when I went, most were close to retiring. I was in my early 40s, and retirement was not on the horizon. Dora and I didn't fully understand the topics in those first couple of lectures, but everyone was so nice, so we stayed.

At some point in the meeting, it just clicked: we *can* invest in real estate. We don't have to fix the toilets and we don't have to manage the property; we can just enjoy the steady passive income with amazing returns while we're still working. What other investments will make you 10–12% annual return, paid out in cash flow month after month?

That's When It Got Exciting

Everyone in Freedom Founders is so friendly, welcoming, and willing to share. Normally, people you don't know are guarded about their finances, but everyone here is the complete opposite. Dora and I kept saying, "Everybody here is so happy. They must be eating something." It wasn't like other dental conventions.

By the end of the first day and a half, we were like, "We're going to enjoy this." There was still plenty that was going over our heads, but we were ready to enjoy the ride.

My husband grew up not having a lot financially. I think that's the root of his workaholic mentality—he feels like he can never make enough money. It made him miss out on a lot in life.

I joined Freedom Founders, in part, to show him that he can make a lot of money on the side. He doesn't have to work all those hours. I wanted him to cut back and join the world as a normal human being.

I didn't convince him of Freedom Founders right away. My in-laws are lawyers who do house flipping. They thought I was falling

> *I joined Freedom Founders, in part, to show him that he can make a lot of money on the side. He doesn't have to work all those hours.*

for a Ponzi scheme. They would sit there at Thanksgiving talking about how I was crazy.

But a year into weekly Freedom Founders meetings, my friends and family noticed that it was the real deal. A couple of my friends joined, too. My husband saw that it was actually paying out, so he started investing small amounts here and there. I encouraged him to listen to the educational modules and to talk to some of the advisors. It was free for him to do as my spouse. I didn't want to push him or question him too much, so I didn't know how committed he was until he told me he had invested millions!

With the regular returns, my husband started cutting back at work. He volunteered for fewer shifts and took fewer calls. After ten years of begging, threatening, and yelling about his workload, I never thought he would do it! My friends started seeing him at barbecues and birthdays again. They never saw him before—ever. Now, he was present and showing up on weekends.

Our friends realized that what we were doing must be legitimate if it gave my husband enough peace of mind and passive income to step back from work. And then they started asking about Freedom Founders. I went from being seen as crazy to being a savvy investor!

As an immigrant family, your parents have a lot of insecurities about money that they pass down to you, especially if they start from nothing. My parents had a lot of money previously, but when they came to the US, they had nothing. They had to start from scratch at age forty.

There was always a sense of not having enough security in my family. The way my parents handle money and investing is super conservative; they never think outside of the box. They couldn't afford to lose anything, and they didn't trust the banks. At least in the stock market, there is safety in the fact that everybody does it. It's mainstream. But Freedom Founders sounded like Willy Wonka to my family.

I ended up refinancing one of my mom's rental homes that she bought in cash. That's such an Asian thing to do: buy everything in cash, and accumulate no debt. But my mom has really opened up in the past couple of years. My brother has started investing in a couple of things, too. My Freedom Founders membership has ended up touching a lot of people.

It's hard to be the one family member going against the grain, but I've always had this desire to do things a little differently. At the middle school science fair, when everyone was making volcanoes using baking soda, I did my project on cockroaches!

So I was on board to look outside the box for financial help. Another thing that attracted me to Freedom Founders was the assurance from all the members that it would only take a little time. I spent an hour on it per week. In the little time I had, I was able to easily learn the material, book phone calls with advisors, and talk through it all with my friend Dora. Dora and I would talk with advisors, an hour at a time, and if we were really interested in investing, we'd call them back. It was so fun and fascinating. I love learning and trying new things.

Finally, I Had Control of My Finances

In a short while, I felt in control of my finances. I knew what I was doing. I could predict the returns on my investments. I truly geeked out, spending more and more time on it, because it was so interesting and rewarding.

I started by making small investments, then converted all of my retirement from stock market platforms to a self-directed platform. I completely revamped all my finances after understanding how much I was making annually and how much my practice was making. I was actually paying attention.

I figured out my Freedom Number with David on Blueprint Day, and how much I needed to invest to make it happen. I thought I'd never make it because, with the stock market, you never know how long it's going to take for you to reach a certain dollar amount. With Freedom Founders, you know what you're making every year. You can calculate when it will double for you. Nothing is 100 percent, but it was looking like I could get to my Freedom Number.

Dora and I never anticipated that we could potentially walk away from our practices in our mid-40s. We're both still young, and I don't know if we necessarily want to stop working altogether. We wanted to walk away from the stress of being solely reliant upon our dentistry for income.

Neither of us is working less right now, but we are happier at work because we're not forced to be there. We know that we could walk away from it tomorrow if we wanted to. We are free to hire an associate or stop coming in on Fridays. We have the choice, and when you have the choice, you're not stressed out. We laugh things off, we don't pinch pennies, and we no longer stress about the little details. The pressure is gone.

I've been able to use my Freedom Founders education to improve my relationships with everyone at my practice. David encourages us to think about how we can make our staff feel fulfilled, so I ask my team, *What are your dreams? What do you want to do? What motivates you?* I can share knowledge with them, like how to save for college. Getting to know them better, showing them I care, and helping them achieve their goals makes me feel good, and makes them feel loyal to me as a boss.

Since Freedom Founders, I have had the freedom to prioritize my happiness, and not compromise it. The immigrant mentality is to work as much as you can and spend as little as possible. I was in the habit of compromising on little things that I wanted, like not ordering an expensive appetizer at a restaurant. I now have the assurance that I can truly afford to enjoy life.

A Resurrected Family Life and Freedom

We're less stressed as a family. I also took my kids' college fund completely out of the stock market and put it into alternatives. We are going to be able to meet our savings goals, pay for our kids' college, and have extra on top of that. Even if something happens, we know we will be okay. We don't feel constrained.

I also have time for activities other than work and caring for my kids. My daughter takes piano lessons, and recently I've been inspired to play a little piano too, as I did when I was younger. I've always been athletic and outdoorsy, and now I have time to exercise at Orange Theory. I've just completed my 300th class. It's important that I make fitness a priority with my lupus diagnosis. I work out consistently, which I never had time to do before.

I've realized that I have to make room in my life to do things by hiring people to help me, so I've hired a nanny who cooks and helps out a couple of times per week. And I love traveling. Before having kids and my practice, I traveled abroad every year. During COVID, we traveled locally around California every two or three weeks.

Reading David's books and materials reminded me of how much I loved reading. I've started listening to audiobooks again.

Freedom means having the time and space to get back into some of my favorite hobbies.

For most of us in life, you grow up and go to work. Very few people get the freedom of making money without putting in the hours. The traditional Asian expectation is to be a doctor, lawyer, or accountant because it will make good, stable money. Because of this need for financial stability, Asian immigrant parents generally tend not to ask their kids, "What are you passionate about? What would you like to do to help people?" It's exciting that I can teach my kids at an early age that they can have a career that they're passionate about—not because it's stable, but because it brings them joy.

Whenever my friends or family say they want to work less, worry about the stock market, or express curiosity about another way of life, I tell them that they have options. They don't have to be stressed. They can spend more time with their kids. I encourage them to get their feet wet by making small investments. I break it down for them because I want them to have the same freedom I have. My kids are too young to understand these concepts, but one day I will share them with them, too.

Freedom Founders is almost like college: you can pursue what you're interested in and attend lectures with like-minded people who are eager to learn. For example, the takeaway of the most recent lecture was to let your next calling come to you; don't force it. That's where Dora and I are at now.

I'd love to work with kids through volunteer or mission work. We're in the early stages of figuring out how best to use our money to this end. It's exciting to think about a passion project. In the meantime, I'm teaching my friends and family what I've learned so far.

I've been in the group for two and a half years. It's amazing what a difference just two years makes. Instead of experiencing a midlife crisis, I've experienced a midlife opportunity.

David's group isn't just about making passive income for yourself. It's about making passive income so you can contribute to the world with your newfound time and money.

There's so much more to life than being on life's hamster wheel. David and everyone in the group really cares; their true purpose isn't just making money. They want to leave a legacy for the next generation, and I think that's what gives life meaning.

GETTING THE BAND BACK TOGETHER
DAVID'S TAKEAWAYS:

Audrey Sheu was always a bit of a renegade. Her contrarian nature conflicted with her family's Asian culture that espouses hard work and saving with no specific goal in mind—a mindset of "there can never be enough."

Getting the band back together for Audrey revolved around her appreciation for orchestrating her own financial future through alternative investments. She feels more confident, which has taken the uncertainty and stress out of her financial planning. In addition, her hardworking husband Mark has also been bitten by the self-directing investment bug and has become a more regular "band participant" with the family.

While there is no urgency in the immediate future for retirement, having a definitive plan allows Audrey to enjoy more free time, focusing on areas of her life and family that weren't always possible pre-Freedom Founders. Volunteering, mission trips, and sharing a freedom mindset with her children has become a strong passion that allows for more contribution, purpose, and meaning in her life.

CHAPTER 8

DR. CODY AND HAILEY COWEN

David talks about the necessary "nose to the grindstone" part of everyone's career. I was no exception. After graduating LSU Dental School—where I met my wife, a hygienist—in 2005, we moved to my hometown of Shreveport, Louisiana, bought a new house, and got married, while I started as an associate in another practice.

I joined Dr. Dies, who had been practicing for about ten to fifteen years. He was a smart, honest, hardworking businessman who taught me that dentistry is more than tending to teeth: it's about tending to people. With him, I learned how to work with people, and how to lead.

I was working six days a week, soaking up everything I could. I was eager to not only practice the clinical side of dentistry but to also learn the business side. I wanted to learn; I couldn't get enough of it.

It may sound overwhelming, but I'm a high-energy person, so working six days wasn't a problem for me. Even during the grindstone years, I always carved out time for taking the family to the beach or to the mountains, and for trying new things like scuba diving. We didn't have a ton of weekends for lounging around on the couch, but we're a tight-knit, "work hard, play hard" type of family.

Working by myself was never something I really wanted to do, and I've been lucky that I've never had to. I think if you practice by yourself, your burnout rate is a lot higher. Dr. Dies and I grew our practice into five practices by working hard together over time. When we had filled up for three months, we expanded into another office. As dental school students graduated, they'd come to work for us. I didn't know much about Dental Service Organizations (DSOs) back then; we just grew out of necessity.

The book *The E-Myth* says that we all have an internal business leader inside us, divided into three: a technician, a manager, and a visionary, or entrepreneur. My partners in Shreveport and I fit these descriptions naturally. Dr. Dies, the founding dentist, was the manager. He was a natural at implementing the systems to grow the practice, and he was great with people. Our other partner was the technician: he would work eight days a week digging ditches if he had to. He had that hard-working mentality nailed down. I was the entrepreneur type.

Practice Growth Led to Non-stop Work

A few years into it, I saw that we were growing and could afford to take some days off. I did eventually cut my six-day-a-week schedule down to five, and then four. I didn't want my boys to grow up without me. We noticed that in taking a day off, our profits did not go down, so we restructured our business toward that.

But about twelve years into the Shreveport practice, my wife had grown homesick for her native southern Louisiana. We prayed about what it would mean to move closer to family. We consulted friends and family and thought about how the move would affect our two young boys, who today are ages 13 and 15.

Ultimately, I decided to sell my portion of the Shreveport practice to my two dental partners at the time. Being well into my career at that point, it was stressful to make the move. It was a tough decision to sell the practice; we had a good thing going, and our path was set.

But by networking with friends I had gone to school with, I connected with my current dental business partner, Dr. Michael Juban. He had a thriving, state-of-the-art practice in Baton Rouge with an excellent reputation. He told me if I moved down to Baton Rouge, I could join his practice. So, that's what we did.

The move was a good decision for my wife, my kids, and me. I partnered with Michael, and soon we opened up a second practice. Michael is not only a great business partner but also my best friend. Whether we're in the office during the week or at the golf course on the weekend, we always have a good time.

When I switched practices, I knew that I didn't want my money to be solely dependent on how many hours I worked. So, when I wasn't in the office, I dabbled in real estate.

I had successfully sold my Shreveport practice and was in the process of growing the Baton Rouge practice. I felt confident that I could make some wise real estate investments, but if I had known then what I know now, I would have approached it differently.

Real Estate without Guidance and Knowledge Is an Expensive Education

I ended up buying an affordable block of houses in an LLC with a couple of my friends, but we didn't do our research about that part of town and the amount of turnover from the previous homeowner. The properties haven't cost us any money, but they haven't had cash flow either. I was very debt-averse.

I got a little too brazen and didn't do my due diligence in my first rental properties. We had a flood in 2016. I did have flood insurance, but it was $75,000 in damages that was just cash out of my pocket. I didn't know how much to save for vacancies, utilities, maintenance, and repair.

Regarding the stock market, the traditional "put your money in the stock market, let it grow, get a big nest egg, and go to Monte Carlo" thing never resonated with me. I'm not going to try to save $20 million and live off of 3 percent in Monte Carlo.

After reading the book *Profit First*, by Mike Michalowicz, I created a way to earn passive income from my practice. My partner and I determined a certain amount of profit that each of us would get paid before rent, lights, and utilities. We know what's coming to us every month, so whether I work 20 days in a month or zero, that passive income is there. I try not to touch any of it while I'm working, so I know what I can count on when I'm not working.

But I was seeking more ways to produce reliable passive income that wasn't tied to my business.

I found the answers in Freedom Founders.

I met David by accident while he was speaking at an event for practice management. He was set to discuss his wealth-building strategies to retire in three to five years, focusing on cash flow. It was exactly what I was looking for. That was in 2019.

After hearing David speak at that event, I planned to attend the next Freedom Founders meeting. Then COVID hit.

I had wanted to meet everyone in person, but when that wasn't possible due to COVID, I attended the virtual event in the fall of 2020. I came in as a guest and joined on day two. I met all the FIT captains and hit the ground running.

I had this chunk of my retirement that I didn't know what to do with. I didn't want to put it into the stock market; I had seen it dip and come back during COVID. I wanted to put it into cash flowing investments but didn't know how.

Freedom Founders Guided and Educated Me

But beyond investment strategies, the network and the accountability that Freedom Founders provides have been life-changing. Everybody helps everybody.

When I attended my first Freedom Founders virtual event, I was paying down investments quickly, and not leveraging them. I've since shifted my philosophy to not be so debt-averse, and to use the cash flow to not only fund my retirement but also to keep investing to propel my financial freedom.

My wife agrees with the Freedom Founders way of thinking, too. It really clicked for her on Blueprint Day, when the two of us sat down with David and his wife, Kandace.

We talked about our past, our future goals, our kids, and the practice. We discussed what I currently have, if I wanted to keep practicing, what I wanted to change, what was working for us, and what wasn't. David talked, we listened, and Kandace occasionally chimed in. We didn't talk specific numbers until the last hour of the day when Kandace slipped us a piece of paper with a road map tailored to our exact assets and goals.

David told me that I needed to be more laser focused with my investment approach and less scattered. I had multiple balls in the air, with several real estate properties and multiple dental practices. I was figuring it out as I went along. Now that I've learned so much with Freedom Founders, I better understand how it all works. I have a goal, and I see the path to actualizing it.

Freedom Founders' FIT calls are incredibly helpful for account-ability. As a visionary entrepreneur type, I have a lot of plans, but implementing them has never been my strong suit. I like to hand the ball off to someone and then move on to the next thing. A financial advisor will check in with you once a quarter, but checking in more regularly with Freedom Founders has made me slow down, answer questions, and figure out how to implement my goals. Freedom Founders keeps me focused.

David does all the vetting, but I take the time to educate myself on the investments in my free time. I have a bookkeeper with my practice, so once a month we look at my spreadsheet together. We examine my cash flow, return percentages, and decide if I want to reinvest or move anything around. It's fun.

I'm 42, so I'm relatively young for the group. A younger person may choose not to get involved because you do need a pretty big injection of capital in the beginning. It just worked out for me because of the sale of my practice.

But I wasn't Free for Life™. I wanted a path to get to where I wanted to be. I'm now on that path.

I've deployed into different asset classes. I've talked to my business partner about bringing in additional dental associates to mentor and help take more of the workload. We just hired one who starts in two weeks. That frees my partner and me up to work just a few days a week together; we like doing big cases and implants.

I Still Love Dentistry but under My Terms and Conditions

Dentistry is still a part of my purpose, and I still enjoy getting up and doing it. The massive cash flow from Freedom Founders has allowed me to create a schedule that works for me. I'm able to be

82

selective about the associates we hire. But I don't want to grow to so many practices that quality control becomes difficult.

Ideally, as I get older, I'd like to have two or three practices that I grow with my colleagues. Last year, we hired an associate who is one of our good friends, and soon we'll hire a student who has been shadowing me for the past five or six years. Working with people you know creates a "mom and pop" feel to the work.

Everyone's "Free for Life™" looks different. My wife and I have always tried to make sure that we never put money over our family.

Fortunately, I'm in a position where if I want to take a 10 percent pay cut next year and take two days off a week, I can. I don't have to rely solely on the number of days in the office. I can use my capital assets with real estate and passive income from my practice, and I still have stocks, bonds, and retirement accounts, which I'll use when I'm 60, plus life insurance and infinite banking.

Having all these things together has reduced what I thought I needed to do to successfully provide for my family. All these things being in place and cash flowing has removed stress, allowed me to cut back on hours, and go to my kids' football games.

I like driving my son to his 7 a.m. workouts four days a week. He's fifteen years old, training for football, and I like that he sees that I'm right there with him, working hard. I have three half days per week, so I can pick him up from school as well. That's what freedom is to me.

Three years ago, I was working 8 a.m. to 5 p.m. The practice was my main source of income. I was completely focused on growing it and making it more efficient. Even though I don't use the income from my investments right now, I keep growing them. I don't feel burnt out by dentistry. When I'm ready to retire, I will.

Everybody gets to a point where they feel they've contributed to society with their profession and are ready to hang out with their kids and grandkids. I will get to that point when I'll be able to get up and go to Colorado for six weeks with my wife and kids. I'm not there yet; my kids are still 13 and 15.

Until my youngest graduates high school, I would like for them to see me get up and go to work every day. I would like them to value the fact that I'm working to provide for them. It's normal for Dad to wake up and have a cup of coffee—not just go to the golf course. I don't want them to think it's all going to be easy. They will have a period of sacrifice too, after graduation. We've all got to start somewhere and gather experience.

I do hope my kids join Freedom Founders one day. It's so beneficial. The biggest question people have with Freedom Founders is, "What's the catch? You guys talk about 10–15 percent returns and retiring with cash flow, so what's the catch?" My kids have seen how it works for me. They know they don't have to just put savings into a 401(k) and ETFs. They will choose their own path, and I'll be there to answer questions along the way.

Realistically, I see myself practicing dentistry for at least another five years. Even after retirement, I will stay busy. I've never really sat still; I like having multiple irons in the fire. One day I may run out of energy, but not anytime soon!

I'm growing in my freedom journey. Eventually, I will volunteer more with Freedom Founders, make more capital investments, and pursue entrepreneurial ventures.

In terms of paying it forward to the new members of Freedom Founders, I was wary about being a FIT captain because my team captain was so knowledgeable and diligent. I thought I couldn't fill his shoes. But I ended up co-captaining with Dr. Ben Jensen, who is very easy to work with and synthesizes information so impressively. It's fun to talk to new members and those who are ready to retire.

Because Freedom Founders convenes at fantastic destinations, my family has been tailoring our vacations around the meetings. Dallas, Puerto Vallarta, Amelia Island, Puerto Rico, Lake Tahoe— you name it. It's been great to get involved in the community that way. There's nothing better for education than being around people with like-minded goals.

I'm very grateful not just for David, but for all the people that work at Freedom Founders: David, Alex, Lindsay, Nathan, the Trusted Advisors, and all the members. It's a big commitment to stay as involved as they have. It has definitely changed my life.

GETTING THE BAND BACK TOGETHER
DAVID'S TAKEAWAYS:

Like the other hardworking and high-caliber Freedom Founders members, Dr. Cody Cowen is non-traditional— a contrarian in many ways. He found that the framework for creating financial freedom (and thus more time) in the Freedom Founders community provided the life-changing next steps that he needed.

Always on his own frontier, Dr. Cowen had tried some real estate investment on his own and, as is typical of Do-It-Yourselfers, realized that his time was best spent providing leadership and mentorship in his dental practices. Freedom Founders provided exactly what he needed to create the passive cash flow to give him options and choices.

For Dr. Cowen, getting the band back together means enjoying more time with his wife and two boys.

Cody wants to be a role model for his sons in terms of work ethic, yet at the same time, to show them that real freedom comes from assets that produce lifestyle income instead of labor. Dr. Cowen intends to continue to practice on his own terms with his partner for at least five more years. My guess is that he will stay involved in dentistry much longer than five years, but in very different ways than even he can visualize right now. Freedom has a way of enhancing creativity.

CHAPTER 9

DR. GREG AND JACKIE LINNEY

It's true what they say—the most valuable things in life aren't material possessions. One of the first things Jackie ever said to me about marriage was that she didn't care about big homes and cars. We met later in life, and by that point, we just wanted to create memories with the kids and travel together.

So, about eight years ago, we decided to start a tradition of family vacations. At the time, the kids would fly in for Thanksgiving, but that was about it and that just wasn't enough. One busy holiday week at home was not going to cut it. However, visiting our kids wasn't a simple matter. They are all in their upper thirties and live all over the country. Our solution was to pay for a week of vacation someplace so that our kids could fly out to our agreed-upon destination. Still, that was only two weeks out of the whole year with our family.

One day, Jackie noticed that our staff was taking more time off than we were. Prior to our daughter's wedding in 2019, we had never taken two weeks off in a row. We had only done three weeks in a given year, but never together.

We were successful, sure, but our lives were totally out of balance. Our practice, located in a wealthy suburb of Houston, was thriving. It was a good practice; our clients were oil executives. But we felt obligated to work so much. We knew it was possible to take more time off, but we didn't know how.

At the time, we had all our money in the stock market and in our pension plan. We knew we would sell the dental practice at some point, but I didn't feel comfortable putting the lump sum from the sale of the practice into the stock market as well. I didn't want it in the same place as our other money. Plus, the broker we spoke to said we would have to live on 4 percent of our retirement. Even though we were good savers, I looked at the math, and realized we would need to majorly ratchet down our lifestyle—and we weren't even doing much then besides working. It didn't look good.

I had read an article by David Phelps around this time. He said it was possible to get 10–12 percent annualized investment returns instead of drawing down 4 percent (the traditional financial model). That would *double* our retirement income. It would be life-changing.

It All Sounded Too Good to Be True

Was it really possible? I knew there were horror stories about dentists making bad investments, and then having to work long past the appropriate retirement age. When I was a young dentist, I met an 83-year-old practicing dentist. He told me he had made a bad investment in a shopping center and lost all his money years ago. He advised me to just stick with what I know—dentistry—and not get caught up in any schemes.

So, I put my blinders on. I worked diligently practicing dentistry for thirty-seven years, at times losing 20 percent, 30 percent, and even 40 percent in the stock market's cycles. We did buy one property in Houston, but we ended up selling it a year and a half later because of all the maintenance and management required. I didn't know the ins and outs of real estate investing then.

Armed with a hefty dose of skepticism, but led by an even stronger pull of curiosity, Jackie and I found ourselves in Salt Lake City at our first Freedom Founders meeting just two weeks after reading that article about David Phelps. Jackie did not want to go; the whole thing sounded too good to be true. She absolutely insisted that I not sign anything once we got there.

Yet, after the first day, her tune changed. She told me, "If you don't sign on the dotted line, I might kick your ass."

Now, I'm a numbers person, but Jackie is highly perceptive at reading people. I don't go all in on something unless she trusts it. At the first meeting, she spoke candidly with all the significant others to decipher if this was the real deal. By the end of the evening, she told me, "Greg, I talked with spouse after spouse. It's real."

> She told me, "If you don't sign on the dotted line, I might kick your ass."

Once I had crunched the numbers and felt that trust was established, it was a no-brainer to join. It was our ticket out. We took all our money out of the stock market and invested it according to the Freedom Founders' guidance.

Starting in January of 2019, we were able to take nine weeks off from work without skipping a beat. When we returned, our practice was busier than ever, with a three-to-six-month waiting period to see patients. We had established trust with them, and it was wonderful not to worry about them leaving us just because we desperately needed a break.

Around this time, I was diagnosed with prostate cancer, but as I was dealing with that, we had already begun earning passive income thanks to Freedom Founders. What could have been an extremely rocky time personally and financially was a smooth and comfortable transition. I'm so thankful to say that I am now healthy, and we're living the dream.

Life is short, and you've got to make the best of everything you've got. If something horrible happens, it will either be a good story later, or we'll learn something in the process—even if we don't understand why in the moment.

So, we figured that we would sell the practice and leave Freedom Founders after our term was up. We had sold the practice: the deal was set to close on March 31st, 2020. Of course, COVID changed everything. The buyer backed out. Selling the practice did take longer than we anticipated, but that delay meant we were reaping the benefits of Freedom Founders before we had even retired.

Because we knew we were going to sell the practice eventually, we shut down our pension plan. We took all of that money and invested it before we even sold the practice. I understood the Freedom Founders concepts, and I trusted the process. Once I'm in, I'm all in.

It was the smartest move we could have made. The first couple of weeks after those major financial moves, I was a bit nervous—but three months after our initial investments with Freedom Founders, I was already getting passive income before retiring. While the COVID downturn in the stock market made our friends lose millions, checks were coming in the mail for us. I was at the end of my career, and COVID could have thrown all our plans and savings down the drain. It could have completely ruined my retirement.

Knowledge without Action Is Useless

I acted upon the information from Freedom Founders at the perfect time, and we didn't have to do or change a whole lot. It was such a comfort knowing that there were people putting out tremendous information while everybody else was panicking. The wealth of knowledge that they supplied to us ahead of our retirement, and ahead of the COVID downturn, was invaluable. It put us ahead of everybody. We knew we could survive whatever the future had in store for us.

If I hadn't stumbled upon Freedom Founders, I would have pulled the practice off the market in 2020 out of fear. I would have lost everything in the stock market.

But because of Freedom Founders, we were sitting at home in the middle of COVID, looking at each other and realizing, "You know what? This is awesome. We're ready for retirement. Our money is going to support us." It's not that we hated running the dental practice—we just realized we had done enough. We were ready for the next chapter of our lives.

Freedom Founders has taught us that there are so many ways to invest and earn a passive income. After Freedom Founders, we realized we could afford our home outside Houston and a second place in Palm Springs. There is no more constant worry about the stock market. Even with rising inflation, we never have to be at its whims again.

We have fully replaced my salary, and our Palm Springs property will be worth so much more in 40 years. A house may drop 10%, but it's not going to drop 40% like the stock market.

Before age 62, I never understood the concept of passive income. But I'm thankful I learned now, because it has changed our lives, and it will make our kids' lives better, too. We will teach our kids that it's not about being filthy rich or having a big home. It's about the freedom to get away, make memories, and enjoy peace of mind. We will teach our kids how to achieve what we've achieved. As the saying goes, "If you give a man a fish, you feed him for a day. If you teach a man to fish, you feed him for a lifetime."

When you are running a practice full-time, you don't have the mental space to think about the big picture. You have little chunks of time here and there, but you don't truly have the time to act on what's important to you.

Now, we have the freedom to travel and make memories with our family. We have time to mentor young people personally and financially. We enjoy investing. We play as much golf as we want. We enjoy our two homes. We are letting a new structure for our lives take shape organically.

Jackie and I are writing a book about our journey called *If You Only Knew*. It started as a legacy book for our children, but it has transformed into something bigger.

We admit that we seemingly have it all—a happy marriage, loving family, secure finances—but it wasn't always this way for either of us. Having survived many challenges before we met, and even more afterward, we know the work that goes into building a life of joy. Oftentimes, if we only knew what others have been through, we might rethink our assumptions about their "easy" lives.

Every human has felt like a misfit, an outlier, a victim. But what if we didn't have to feel that way forever? Life is rarely easy, but it can always be joyful. You just have to know the right formula to achieve it. In *If You Only Knew*, readers learn how to rewire their thinking to choose honesty and gratitude and to program themselves for a life of resiliency, laughter, and love.

We wouldn't be writing it at all if it weren't for Freedom Founders. Our membership in this group enabled us to take this journey that has given us the money, time, and mental bandwidth necessary to live and to tell our story.

In fact, writing had been my greatest fear. I have a learning disability, which makes me a slow reader. So, the process was quite intimidating. Having the time to face my fear and tackle this challenge has been extremely rewarding. Jackie had a premonition years ago that we would write a book together, and it's finally coming to fruition.

It has also been very rewarding to co-captain and teach the freshmen in Freedom Founders. Jackie and I value tremendously the friendships and connections formed in the group. We love watching their reactions when the new members first see the money coming in. It's a thrill every time to witness them let go of their legitimate skepticism, trust the process, and trust the group. It's a uniquely warm group atmosphere because the trust is so real and so earned. The *a-ha* moments and the successes just keep coming.

Jackie and I are Free for Life™, but we're still involved in Freedom Founders. We are big believers in paying it forward. I tell my mentees that the new people coming in are sitting right where they were three months ago. I encourage them to get to know the new people, to tell them not only about their successes but also their doubts. Just when you think you've learned it all, the exchange of information, stories, and guidance from multiple generations never cease to be exciting.

You come into Freedom Founders thinking it's about investments, and it is—but what you gain is so much more. You gain camaraderie and trusted friends for life. That's the real prize.

Jackie's Insight and Wisdom

When we got married, I told Greg, *"I don't need a big house or fancy cars. I could live in a small shack as long as we make just enough to keep us happy and make memories."*

That is the most important thing to me: making memories.

Freedom Founders has allowed us to do that. We're able to make memories together without having to worry about finances. Because of Freedom Founders, our yearly family vacations have allowed us to continue our tradition in a way that I never would have envisioned. The trips have become EPIC and have evolved to a point where we are able to fly everyone into and stay in some amazing locations without worrying about the costs. It has become so important even to our adult children who look forward to it every year. So, in a nutshell, Freedom Founders has really allowed MY dreams to come true.

Freedom Founders has also allowed us to create a legacy of mentoring. We love mentoring young couples in both relationships and business. They ask us . . . *"what are you doing financially that you can take these trips and make these memories?"*

I remember when we attended our first meeting, I was skeptical. I didn't necessarily know all about the numbers and the financials. I wanted to talk to the people. I worked the room that first meeting. I talked to every spouse I could. Everyone was very genuine and very honest. My reservations just washed away.

GETTING THE BAND BACK TOGETHER
DAVID'S TAKEAWAYS:

For Greg and Jackie Linney, getting the band back together has meant the freedom that passive income replacement has allowed for time with family, travel, and memories.

As a hardworking traditionalist (work hard, keep your head down, and invest in the stock market, 401(k), etc.), Greg had never understood "passive income." His financial planner advocated for a depletion rate of about 4 percent from their net investment capital, which had Greg feeling uncertain about their lifestyle's future.

Jackie was the skeptic when it came to this "new group" Greg had found that promised financial freedom in 3–5 years. She admits to "working the room" at their first meeting and then telling Greg, "This is real. We need to do this."

Two years later, Greg and Jackie are Free for Life™ members, part of the Frontier Group, and mentors to other members and young people who want to learn the frameworks of freedom and financial advocacy. Getting the band back together means time with family, travel, and cherished memories.

CHAPTER 10

DR. BEN AND SONDRA JENSEN

A dentist's income is certainly a blessing. My wife, Sondra, and I were always good at saving and planning, and Sondra's father gave us extremely helpful financial advice over the years, but we needed help in getting to the next level. That said, everybody we talked to—from financial advisors to stock market "gurus"—either weren't as far along as we were or weren't where we wanted to be. *How can you get to the next level if no one you know is there?*

After graduating from dental school in Minneapolis, I practiced in the Twin Cities for about three years prior to having our first child. Sondra was a working professional there who enjoyed her career as an executive but hated leaving our young son in daycare. Then, one day, she came home distraught: the realization that we'd have to put him in daycare every day had sunken in. Whether she wanted to stay home to watch our son or keep working, I was ready to support her either way.

We asked ourselves: *where do we really want to live to raise our family?* Ultimately, we decided together to move back to our home state of South Dakota, and that she would stay home with our son. We found an amazing little town and an old-school practice in rural South Dakota. I bought it from an older practitioner and expanded it from 800 square feet to 4400 square feet.

For a good twelve or fifteen years, everything was going great. We had always avoided taking on too much debt, and we were able to pay off what debt we did have. Our finances seemed to be in order.

Living in South Dakota means the pace of life is a little bit slower. The dentist who sold his practice to me encouraged me to only work four days a week. At that time, I was working five, but cutting back to four allowed me to spend quality time with my family. That's the kind of life we wanted when we decided to move to South Dakota in the first place. Passing this approach on to the next generation, we have spent the past 20 years encouraging our kids to chase their dreams.

But I wasn't completely happy with just being a dentist. I had reached a point where I wasn't intellectually stimulated, and I was searching for something more. On top of that, we found ourselves frustrated that we couldn't see a clear path to retirement, despite paying off our debts. We were spinning our wheels. Saving up a pile of cash and then depleting it in retirement, hoping we don't outlive it, just never made sense to us.

Around that time, I started listening to David's podcasts and educating myself about real estate and other ways to create my own freedom. But nothing resonated with me the way David's podcast did.

So I went through the interview process to see if I would be a fit to attend an in-person Freedom Founders conference. David extended the invite. The next step was convincing my wife.

Skeptical and Unsure but Willing to Check It Out

As Sondra tells it, "I was skeptical. I was willing to attend on the condition that we would not sign up for any membership, commit to anything, or buy anything whatsoever. We were just there to check it out.

"Once we got there, it was a different story. We had found a group of people that we really fit in with. The message David relayed in his podcast translated into a rewarding culture and a fully-fledged community."

We absorbed all the information that Thursday and Friday of the conference. By Saturday, we checked in with each other: *Is this a group we actually want to move forward with? Did we feel the same way about it?* Sondra looked at me and said, "I think we've found our community. I think we should do this."

Needless to say, I was happily surprised we were completely on the same page. Freedom Founders was the first group we came across that was *ahead* of where we wanted to be, and they knew what we needed to do to get there.

After attending our first meeting in 2017, we decided to commit to Freedom Founders for one year. We considered it an investment in our education. We were curious where the journey could take us.

A general curiosity, intellectual restlessness, and a need for a clear path to retirement led me to Freedom Founders, rather than the desperate need to retire immediately. We took our time learning as much as we could at our pace. We also didn't end up doing our Blueprint Day until about a year after our first meeting—later than the average members.

That's when we met with David and his wife Kandace over a weekend at their Dallas home. We did our homework in advance, summarizing where we were and where we wanted to go, and we combed through all the investments Sondra and I had made over the past decade. In return, they pushed us to figure out how we could be more efficient, working less time and still bringing home the same amount of income. We evaluated how hard we wanted to chase income versus quality of life, and how much time our boys have left with us.

We were ready for David and Kandace to give us a laundry list of all the ways we could improve. But by the middle of the second day with them, David said, "You're practically there." It was just a matter of redeploying our existing assets to create cash flow. We were poised to replace my earned income with passive income. That was the number I was aiming for.

It blew my mind: I had no idea we were so close to achieving freedom. By age 44, I was already that close to actually having many more options in my life than I had ever dreamed of. It was eye-opening and incredibly exciting.

> David said, "You're practically there." It was just a matter of redeploying our existing assets to create cash flow.

But even more impactful than that was David's suggestion that I cut back to a three-day workweek, so I tried it out when I returned home. The very next week, I took off an extra day.

After a few months of implementing this extra free time in my week, I had a newfound perspective on my practice and on my life.

I was feeling genuine freedom. With a four-day work week, I tended to think about work even when I wasn't working; having that extra day meant I could truly decompress on the weekends. It was a game-changer for me personally, but most of all for us as a family.

The feeling of freedom is much more satisfying than hitting a certain number. It allowed me to take the time to smell the roses, which is the true embodiment of success. I have learned the distinction between *achieving* success, which is a grind and *feeling* successful, which is pure enjoyment.

Within a couple of months of our Blueprint Day, we had met the monthly numbers of cash flow that we needed; we were Free for Life™. In the fall of 2019, we had our Free for Life™ ceremony. I credit David and Kandace for opening our eyes to seeing that we were nearly already there. David positioned us to execute our goals. And I credit my father-in-law, Gary, for giving Sondra and me a stellar foundation of financial understanding, which put us in the position to be able to consider Freedom Founders in the first place.

Freedom is just the beginning. Ever since our move back to South Dakota all those years ago, we have always tried to prioritize time with our boys. We didn't want to miss events. We wanted to be present.

I have the luxury of being married to a woman who keeps me grounded. Together we make decisions that prevent me from getting too lopsided in my priorities. Our priorities have always been our kids and our faith. We didn't want money to be the driver of our life.

Freedom Founders pointed us to a better path toward retirement and gave us the tools and resources to do it ourselves.

I should say that we had been passionate about investing before Freedom Founders. I was always eager to learn about the next great investment opportunity. We had put quite a bit into the stock market. I had taken real estate courses and had done some multi-family and hotel syndication deals, and dabbled in venture capital investments. We invested mostly traditionally, either qualified or non-qualified investments and mutual funds. We were heavily focused on investments that were almost strictly growth and didn't actually create cash flow. That meant we didn't feel their benefit in our day-to-day lives. It was all in the name of saving for later.

In this dabbling, there is minimal education involved. You trust a stockbroker to choose stocks that will grow over the next two or three decades until you're ready to retire. You choose 3 percent or 4 percent to live on each year, depending on your standard of living. We didn't know what our wealth could do for us or how to manage it personally; we were abdicating the responsibility. That's normal for investing, and that's okay, but we had zero control of the outcomes. Fortunately for us, these growth investments tended to work out quite well. We did not have a history of losing our shorts in any investment. Sure, we made some investments that I wouldn't make again today, and we lost some money along the way, but we managed to avoid life-altering catastrophes.

In my dabbling, we had attended other conferences before Freedom Founders. But the thing that made us get on board with Freedom Founders was the fact that we would do it ourselves. We weren't handing off our savings to someone else. Someone wasn't selling us more products or investments. Instead, David and his team were sharing the tools, and we would use them. Most importantly, the mentorship was built in—people who had already successfully done what we wanted to do would guide us.

So many deals out there in the "real world" are one-sided, benefitting chiefly the dealmaker. But David carefully vets his Trusted Advisors, which removed the roadblock we had of finding trustworthy guides on our own. David had already gone through that process and spent a lot of time finding good quality people who offered fantastic investments. It was exactly what we had been needing. The power of all our resources together creates good interest rates, good teams, and good returns. It's a synergy unlike anything we had seen before.

The Passive Income Cash Flow Model Made So Much Sense

Prior to Freedom Founders, the biggest problem I had with my financial advisor was the accumulation model. It's counterintuitive for me to build up a stockpile of wealth and spend the rest of my days spending it down. It would keep me in a conservative mindset, always saving, forever. Not an ideal plan.

The passive income cash flow model made so much more sense to me, and that's what Freedom Founders offers. You're accumulating assets that only appreciate in the future, not just stocks. There's both growth *and* cash flow. When I do decide to stop dentistry, that cash flow will sustain us.

Financial advisors ask the impossible question of when we will die. No one knows! So it's impossible to know how much money you can really afford to spend every year—the typical 3–4 percent, or even 2 percent if you live past 90. Not a good long-term strategy, especially when you factor in inflation, taxes, and other uncontrollable world events.

Most of all, instead of spending down my retirement, I wanted something to transfer to the next generation. The hard work Sondra and I do is not for the sole benefit of ourselves. Our kids are our driving force that gives meaning to everything. It's all for them.

As you're living off the cash flow, the asset continues to grow in value, which means your wealth and cash flow continue to grow with you as you age. These assets also increase with inflation, irrespective of any political climate. The underlying growth in the assets means that your cash flow grows even as the cost of living rises.

In parallel with redeploying our assets, we were also put into a Freedom Implementation Team (FIT) group. The FIT group has weekly calls with other members on the same level as you. My group really pushed each other. It's a culture of learning, and I'm an information junkie. I love learning new things. But even better are the relationships formed in my FIT group; we've become very close friends. We got to know each other better at subsequent events, and then a group of four of us started having our own weekly calls. We pushed and challenged each other's status quo regularly.

I came into Freedom Founders wanting to grow *financially*, but the *personal* growth for me has been tremendous, too. Growing relationships wasn't even on my radar. But the whole group has affected me personally, professionally, and even in my faith, for the better.

Being Free for Life™ has improved my overall attitude about life. I'm more relaxed during my quality time with my family. I'm no longer on the endless hamster wheel. Everything has more meaning.

Sondra and I enjoy being able to better focus on our personal lives since I cut my workweek down from four days to three. Sondra has had the time to co-chair the fundraising committee for a $2.5 million community soccer project.

Per Sondra: "Our boys gained so much from our hometown soccer community, and we wanted to give back. Even though our kids won't directly benefit from this work, future kids will enjoy it. It's fun to give back to something that so many other local families here will use for generations to come."

I'm proud of Sondra for taking it on, and prior to Freedom Founders, she wouldn't have had the bandwidth. I also find it extremely rewarding to use some of the extra time that I have now to continue to help others who are a step or two behind me on this journey. I get to participate in FIT calls with the freshman class now. It feels so meaningful to be able to guide others the way David guided me.

David talks about five freedoms: financial, relational, time, freedom of purpose, and health. I've really gained so much more from Freedom Founders than just financial freedom. Having this extra day in the week has given us time to actually work on some of the things that we find meaningful, and one of those things is being able to give back to the Freedom Founders community that has done so much for me in these past five years. I look forward to every opportunity to talk to anyone who has questions or wants to know how we did it. I'm glad to share—I've been a FIT captain for several years.

We Now Have the Tools and Confidence to Invest in Real Estate

David gave us the tools and the education to feel confident in our ability to invest and to create a growing passive income that will continue to sustain us. Despite some uncertain market forces, I feel certain of our trajectory based on how we have positioned ourselves financially.

We live in small-town America, so for better or for worse, future economic impacts like inflation are going to hit home. These market cycles only create wealth for those who are prepared. Being in a group like Freedom Founders at a time when there's a lot of uncertainty in the marketplace and in the world makes us feel prepared for whatever is coming.

The power of the group is pretty tremendous. Having a lot of really smart people to bounce ideas off of when the going gets tough makes me confident in the fact that we're going to be able to weather any storm. A storm may hit, and we don't always get to choose our circumstances, but we do get to choose our response. I look forward to learning through this market cycle change because I'm prepared.

I had a plan for my life, but God had an even better plan. Right now, God has me right where he wants me. I find myself fortunate to still love a profession that's been really good to us in a lot of ways.

So, what's next? I'm at that age when it could be time to consider a transition of the practice or to bring on an associate. There is a change on the horizon, but I am still enjoying working three days a week with my amazing team. I'm blessed to get to work with them every day. I enjoy going into the office; it's not drudgery for me in any way. I do feel like it's sustainable for me, potentially even long-term.

Sondra and I are planning time away that we honestly hadn't felt the freedom to take prior to this. Whether I keep practicing or sell my practice, I will be happy.

Having said that, there's a strong pull towards absolute freedom. In a couple of months, we will be empty nesters. We are looking at that transition with a little trepidation, but our kids are certainly ready for the change—probably more ready than we are. Being a parent is the hardest work I'll ever do. It's also the best work I'll ever do.

Freedom Founders asks members to identify their "why." Why spend all this time, money, and energy figuring out retirement and passive income? What is your legacy? My boys are my "why."

Our two boys are now 19 and 21. Our youngest just graduated from high school and is headed off to college in the fall. Our oldest just graduated from college with a business degree. He is set to continue his education as a pilot so that he can fly commercially.

When my oldest son first told me he wanted to be a pilot, I said, "Oh no, you don't want to do that. That's dangerous." After some reflection, I went back to him and said, "If this is something you're talking about doing as a career, I will be supportive of that. Whatever it is that you choose, even if I'm not comfortable with it, I will figure a way to get comfortable with it."

So, I'm following in my son's footsteps: I'm working on getting my private pilot's license right now. The extra time away from work has let me lean into this new challenge, face my personal fear, and ultimately strengthen my bond with my son. He already has his license and is quite a ways ahead of me in his pilot training. I'm still a student pilot, but I'm soloing now and soon I'll be able to fly up to see him and my other son in Minneapolis, which is where they go to school. It's about five hours from us by car, and a little under two hours by plane. I'm looking forward to that. Our kids push us in directions that are unexpected sometimes, and I'm grateful for it.

The most recent Freedom Founders meeting was designed specifically for the next generation. Sondra and I brought both of our boys. It's really amazing when my "why" is literally sitting in the same room with me, and starting to ask some of those same questions that I once was. David's really created a group that cares about legacy.

Now that we have more bandwidth as we're about to be empty nesters, we have more freedom. What does that look like, and what do we want to do with it? It's an exciting time. We're looking at our life and future with new eyes, because when you achieve your dreams, one of the best parts is creating new ones.

Sondra's Insight & Observation

Ben and I had good success at saving money. Our struggle was to find consistent predictable investment opportunities and return on our capital. We utilized two or three consultants in our business. We participated in numerous masterminds over the years, but it was difficult getting to that next step to make our dream of early retirement and transitioning to a freedom lifestyle a reality.

Ben likes change and gets enthusiastic about new opportunities. When he finds something he wants to try, he's passionate about it and all in. I have a more cautious attitude towards change, evaluating the pros and cons of new opportunities. My typical response to Ben's enthusiasm on an idea is, "Hmm, interesting. We'll have to think though that."

I agreed to go with him to our first Freedom Founders meeting, but I mentioned that we were evaluating opportunities for the weekend not signing up for things. I told Ben: "I prefer we not make any big decisions this weekend. We'll come home and evaluate the opportunity together. We aren't doing anything, just listening to the opportunity."

The Freedom Founders meeting blew me away. They were about offering opportunities in education, networking, goal setting, finding options for growth in all aspects of our life, introductions to independent financial opportunities and so much more! I recognized real authenticity in this group. They didn't want to sell us something, they wanted to support our passions and help us achieve OUR goals. This is what we had been looking for. Near the end of the weekend,

I looked over at Ben, smiled and said, "let's do it." Imagine his surprise ...

Freedom Founders has helped us take the next steps in our journey towards freedom. We were able to take the resources we had accumulated and deploy it to create real cash flow. Ben and I built more freedom in our lives by working less while increasing productivity and efficiency allowing us to enjoy more family time. And this is just the beginning ... Thank you, David, we are forever grateful my friend!

GETTING THE BAND BACK TOGETHER
DAVID'S TAKEAWAYS:

Getting the band back together for Dr. Ben Jensen came from increasing his "bandwidth" (more TIME). Instead of at work, he now gets to spend his time with his wife, Sondra, and their two young adult sons.

Attaining Free for Life™ in just eighteen months transformed Ben's practice style. He quickly reduced his workweek from four to three days and found serving patients to be more fun and less stressful. Enjoying active income production is a part of the freedom equation—not the norm for most small business owners.

Sondra, like many of our members' spouses, was quite reluctant to travel to their first Freedom Founders meeting. While she was adamant that they "would not be joining anything," by the second day she told Ben, "We should do this." Once again, female intuition is often needed to confirm a good decision.

The clarity of a real plan obtained on their Blueprint Day, along with the accountability and high curation of investment opportunities, provided Ben and Sondra with what they needed to move away from the traditional financial model of accumulation to one that focuses on passive cash flow. "Culture and a full-fledged community with the necessary tools and resources" was the key to their freedom.

CHAPTER 11

DR. HIRU AND SUMIT MATHUR

Before Freedom Founders, my husband and I had a rental property in Houston that turned out to be the rental from hell. It was a very nice, brand new home in a good location. We had a realtor who was a friend of mine. Because it was so new, she said it wouldn't require a lot of repairs. She screened some tenants and found someone whom she said we didn't have to worry about.

But before long, the tenant was making late payments by five days, then ten days—and every month it was getting worse. After a few months, I couldn't stand it. I did not want to call people and ask them to pay their rent, so I decided to go ahead and find a management company. They concluded that they would have to kick him out. He stopped paying completely once the company took over.

As I was waiting for them to figure out the legalities, I got a Facebook message from someone saying, "Are you the owner of this house? It's in bad shape—the door is open and there's no-body inside."

Shocked, my husband and I drove to the property and, sure enough, our front door was smashed open, there was nobody inside, and everything was a mess. The place was abandoned. We couldn't believe it. I called the cops. The neighbors told us that there was an armed robbery in the house. Turns out, my tenant was a drug dealer!

The robbers had smashed the door when my tenant wasn't home. And then apparently the next morning, the guy packed up a U-Haul and disappeared. The management company didn't know. For three whole weeks, the door was left open with no one inside. I was so upset.

We got the door fixed and found a new tenant. Since then, the company's taken over. It's been resolved, but I never wanted to go through an ordeal like that again. Thankfully, around that time we discovered Freedom Founders, and our life's never been the same—for the better.

Before joining Freedom Founders, my husband, Sumit, and I were very busy with our young boys. We didn't think about anything except work. Now that they've grown up, we have a bit more time and income. We started thinking, *What's our next?*

I was very frustrated with my practice because I felt like it was too much stress on me. I had to perform procedures and shoulder responsibilities that I didn't enjoy. I just wasn't feeling good in life. I was "successful," but I wasn't able to do the things I enjoyed.

So I started seeking out groups and people who I felt would guide me into getting out of dentistry entirely. I thought my path might be to invest in real estate or to find some sort of passive income so that I wouldn't have to depend on the practice. I began researching everything.

We Had Full-Time Jobs, but We Wanted to Build a Stream of Passive Income

First, Sumit and I tried a Tony Robbins training for real estate investments. We quickly realized that it was not for us because we didn't have the time to actively look for deals. We both have our businesses, so we were looking for a way to earn passive income without being actively engaged. Second, we had the rental property from hell.

But just when we started to feel our search was fruitless, we happened to find Freedom Founders on an online dentist forum. People were praising it, so I looked it up and sent a message to David. I got a callback and an invitation to come to one of the events. On our way to the event, I told my husband that I wasn't sure I wanted to join; I just wanted to get a taste of what it was all about. But in the back of my mind, I knew that I would leap on any good path to get out of dentistry. I was just so tired of it.

One of the Freedom Founders mottos that they had was, "Get out of your practice and be free in three to five years." That was my goal. When we went to the event, we were just amazed by the people and by the information. David was clearly such a genuine, knowledgeable, and caring person. We were totally enamored by the whole group.

When I am in my own office, it feels like I'm in a tiny bubble. We periodontists don't always know what's going on outside. We don't talk to each other, and we don't know what other people are doing. It's a very isolating way to work.

David is very careful about who he picks for the group. When we first met the group, they were all ready for us with open arms. We felt so much at home. My husband said, "This is the community we've been looking for." He knew that one of my biggest frustrations was that I was very uninspired by the people around me. It made me feel like maybe I shouldn't do dentistry anymore because no one around me was enjoying it. I couldn't see the positive side of it.

During our Blueprint Day soon after the event, David and Kandace outlined what they felt we were capable of and should be doing. We thought, "Wow, can we actually achieve those things?"

"Of course you can," they said, showing us exactly how. We started our journey to freedom, making investing and lifestyle changes with confidence.

The passive income and financial freedom are great, but the biggest thing I learned from the group was how to find time to do the things I love with the people I love.

Implementing David's Blueprint Day advice meant I was no longer stuck with responsibilities I didn't enjoy. That was my biggest benefit from joining the group. Once I got the passive income, it took the pressure and financial dependence off of my practice. I was free to restructure my practice the way I wanted to. So I focused on what I liked doing and the people I liked to work with.

> ... the biggest thing I learned from the group was how to find time to do the things I love with the people I love.

As I have a referral-based periodontics practice, dentists refer patients to me because I specialize in certain procedures. I was having a hard time with some of the dentists because they were just not good to work with, but now I don't have to depend on the referrals. I stopped marketing to the dentists I didn't want to work with anymore. I got my life back because now I'm focusing on what I enjoy. It massively relieved the pressure.

In addition, right before I joined Freedom Founders in 2019, I fell and fractured my right arm, so there were certain procedures that really hurt my hand. I used to continue doing them because I had no choice, but now I've hired associates to offload some procedures from my plate. Physically, it's been better for my health because I don't have chronic pain from doing too many procedures. I have less pain and more happiness.

I gave myself more time for investing, taking care of my health, and seeing our boys—now 26 and 19—who live in different cities. I actually have time to work out. I can focus on cooking better meals.

If I Had Only Known about Freedom Founders Earlier

There's so much more than just financial freedom; I've gotten my life back. Every day has been like, "Wow, I wish I'd done this earlier!"

In a big hurry to get my finances organized, I've been like a kid in a candy store with all the deals available and vetted, Trusted Advisors to work with. It's been so great to be able to trust them, and know that I could talk with them any time.

When you invest in the stock market, you don't even know the broker. But with Freedom Founders, it's a one-on-one relationship. The advisors are so patient in explaining everything, which is especially helpful in the beginning when you're still learning it all.

There was a lot of learning along the way. I learned by talking to the Trusted Advisors and participating in the weekly FIT group meetings. It's so nice to learn how your peers deal with issues in investing, in life, and in dentistry. It keeps us accountable.

Every week, we talk about what works for us and what doesn't. If we have any questions, David will shoot a video right away and send it to us, to explain the answer, or he'll connect us to someone who can give us an answer.

With this community learning, my knowledge about real estate investing has grown tremendously. We read so many books and David introduces us to authors and expert speakers. We attend different events, join different groups, and go on due diligence trips to the Trusted Advisors' area of work to see the homes they invest in, how they build them, and how they conduct their entire business. Once we understand the business, it's easier for us to decide if it's the right investment for us. Through the support of Freedom Founders and the Trusted Advisors, the learning has been easy and simple.

When my husband and I were investing initially, I had more nonqualified funds (taxable accounts) outside of my IRA and Sumit had more funds in his IRA. So we basically decided to invest based on the tax benefits of each. We were not really looking for cash flow because we both work. We were looking for growth.

In Freedom Founders, everything we've invested in is getting reinvested and the profits are going back into the investment, compounding the gains. Most of our investments were in our qualified retirement funds, compounding tax-deferred. The accounts that were outside of our retirement accounts were mostly based on tax benefits and compounding growth. For instance, we've invested more in real estate properties (equities) rather than in lending. Whenever those real estate deals bring us any cash flow dividends, we reinvest it back into more deals.

In the past, we would invest occasionally. Now, we don't let our money sit around. We're constantly thinking about how to make our money work for us. We have this buffet of investments to choose from. Sometimes, I invest in a deal and get my principal back, which I then reinvest right away into something else because I have so many choices. Instead of sitting around and thinking about it, I'm ready to deploy it and make it work for me. We just love that the money works for us so that we don't have to work that hard. We can both just work for fun.

> Now, we don't let our money sit around. We're constantly thinking about how to make our money work for us.

Because I don't have to work for an income, the first thing I did was change my hours. I used to work early and then come home late. Now, I start my first patient at around ten. I'm an early riser, but now I have four or five hours in the morning to ease me into the day. I can meditate, exercise, and take care of myself. When I do that, my entire day goes well. I live with intention instead of running around like crazy. That simple change has made me so happy and calm. I used to dread going to work because I had all these patients lined up.

Now I just look forward to it because I work with my favorite cases and my favorite patients. I have the freedom of working for pleasure—not for money. It's just for my internal happiness. I'm there because I enjoy doing the procedures and I feel very fortunate that I can choose to do that. I go to work, I work on the patients I love, and I do the exams which I enjoy.

I have an incredible amount of happiness because I enjoy dentistry. You see a lot of dentists who don't enjoy it, and for a time, I was one of them. I didn't enjoy rushing from patient to patient. I love talking to patients, getting to know them, and advising them. I felt like I wasn't giving them my best; it wasn't what I signed up for.

Less Stress and More Relaxed

Because I'm less stressed now, it's had positive ripple effects on my team, my family, and my patients. Because I'm not under pressure, I'm not stressing out everyone around me. It's a more relaxed work environment. It's why the practice has grown: because the patients can see how much we are all enjoying it. I used to stress everybody out, from my patients and my staff to my family. Now, everyone's in shock at the change in me because I'm just much happier.

Another change I've made since Freedom Founders is hiring two part-time associates. I decided I wanted to work less, even if it meant losing money, so they took over most of my patients. With my time freed up, I ended up being able to do bigger cases. My income didn't go down and the practice grew. The cash flow increased and I was reinvesting it. So physically, I'm not working as hard, yet my income still hasn't gone down. It's a wonderful situation to be in when you're not actually dependent on the income from the practice, but it's still coming in.

I have time to do other things, too, like teaching. I've been teaching part-time at my alma mater's dental school since 2000, but I would love to shift to mentoring a select few—say four or five people—in my office. I would like to mentor them on how to have a successful practice, how to do dental implants, how to prioritize happiness, and not wait as long as I did to live a better life. Because I've been in this area for almost 20 years, I get asked for advice, but I have been too busy with my practice to mentor on a deep level.

Whether my future mentorship is just clinical, or a combination of lifestyle and clinical, I am excited to teach more going forward.

I also wrote a book during COVID, called *It's All About the Gum*. I strongly believe there's a connection between the body and the mind. I treat gum disease, and there are so many connections between the bacteria, the mouth, and the rest of the body. The book is about how taking care of the gums can actually prevent diseases like Alzheimer's. I wanted to increase awareness of that, and I am hoping to get that message out to everybody by having the book available on Amazon. I want to write more books going forward as well.

My family and I also love to travel. I used to take only one week off, maximum, for travel because of the deluge of patients waiting for me when I returned. We would try and visit one new country every year. For the past 15 years, that was our tradition, but now I can afford to take more time off because I know my practice is taken care of.

I grew up in India, but my favorite place in the whole world to visit is Italy. I've been there several times and I cannot get enough. I love Europe, especially France and Greece. We've also been to Brazil, Argentina, Thailand, Vietnam, Egypt, Costa Rica, Hawaii, and Alaska. Going on international trips as our boys grew up helped to cement their values. We were all so busy at home in our routines, but when you go to a foreign country with nothing else to focus on except being with each other and learning the culture, you grow closer. Our kids learned to get out of their bubble, realize how fortunate they are, and be grateful for what they had.

Next on our travel bucket list is a safari in Africa—we want to climb Mount Kilimanjaro—then see Machu Picchu and experience South Africa, New Zealand, and Australia. I'm hoping to travel more. Now that the kids have grown up, future trips will probably just be my husband and me, but hopefully, the kids can join us, too.

I enjoy local travel as well. We bought a little beach home in Galveston. We go there to just sit and stare at the water and do nothing. It is such a blessing.

Freedom Founders Has Challenged Me to Become a Leader

My husband, Sumit, and I became Freedom Founders members in August of 2019. The group encouraged me to be a FIT captain, which has helped me with my leadership skills and kept me on my toes. It's been wonderful to give back to the community, and it's helped me grow as a person.

The group of people in Freedom Founders elevates you. They never put you down. They are all very down-to-earth. When I see the amazing things they do in their lives, I get inspired to do the same in mine. Whatever I choose to do, they help guide me on how to get there. Everyone goes above and beyond. The friendships have been amazing.

When we went to the first meeting, Sumit was the one who said, "These are your people. This is your tribe. I guarantee you you'll be happy. There's no way you're leaving here without signing up." And he was so right. He comes to most of the events. He's a small business owner, too, so many of these principles can be applied to his business. David recommended a more specialized group for him, so he has branched out and grown in his own career because of Freedom Founders. But mostly, he's just happy that he has a wife who doesn't complain all the time anymore!

When I first joined Freedom Founders, I wanted to sell my practice and leave dentistry behind. Now, I am actually growing my business and more motivated than ever! It's not a burden anymore. Since I'm having fun, I see myself practicing for five more years at least. I'm also moving into a bigger office space in mid-2022. I've created a space there for mentorship training as well.

My boys have also picked up on a few things about Freedom Founders through us to benefit their lives. One is an aerospace engineer in Phoenix and our other son is a bioengineering student at UCLA. Both are good, smart, family-oriented kids. Just like my husband and I were at their age, they are focused on work and not much else.

When one of our sons moved, he bought a condo and got his roommate to help pay the mortgage. He was building an asset without having to pay that much. He started young. We were willing to help with the down payment, but other than that, he got a loan and figured it out for himself. He then taught the process to his roommate, who did the same thing after. It's so cool to see the positive influence of Freedom Founders, not just on us and our kids, but also on the people around us.

Our boys are both interested in investing and want to grow their savings. They've seen how much happier Sumit and I are now. They're learning to look for happiness in work, but also how to set boundaries and define what makes them happy way before we did. They are going to join us at future Freedom Founders events. We are thrilled for them.

I can't even describe all the different freedoms we now enjoy. Financial freedom is just a tiny part of it. The freedom to choose to work the way I want with whomever I want, along with the freedom of time, have been life-changing.

GETTING THE BAND BACK TOGETHER
DAVID'S TAKEAWAYS:

Dr. Hiru Mathur originally came to Freedom Founders with the goal of selling her periodontal practice as soon as possible. But less than three years later, she is enjoying her evolved practice model because she doesn't have to work. She's proud to say: "It's actually fun!"

Hiru and her husband Sumit had tried some real estate investing on their own with not-so-good results. Next up was attending a Tony Robbins "how to be an active investor" conference, where they learned they didn't need a second job with more stress. What they needed was an authentic guide—proven leaders and a community that had a plan that would fit their current lifestyle and respective business careers.

Getting the band back together for Dr. Mathur became returning to the happiness and joy of practice without the obligation or necessity to do it "the old way." She created the margin of replacement (passive) income which allowed her to experiment and make changes to her model that would have previously made her very nervous and more stressed.

CHAPTER 12

DRS. GERTRUDE AND BOB DUBANSKI

Bob and I are both general dentists and, uniquely, a husband-and-wife team at the same practice.

As Bob tells it: "We started in 1986, working our butts off."

Our approach was *bigger is better*, so we expanded as much as we could. Then, in 2018, I injured both of my wrists while I was doing surgery. After that, I wasn't able to do all the work that I was used to doing, so Bob picked up the slack. Fast forward to 2021—three years later—and he was tired. Very tired.

"We had grown a large practice, so the pressure was on me to work more when Gertrude couldn't do as much. I continued on without her. I loved the industry at the time, and still enjoy it to this day, but the pressure of the business side created an environment that I didn't want to work in anymore.

"We had created a monster. Our practice kept getting bigger. We were beyond the enjoyment of it. It wasn't working for us. I was taking just one week off a year. And even then, I was still thinking about the practice."

Then, when COVID hit, we realized our practice could be shut down overnight. We thought, *What kind of control do we really have?*

None, it turns out, because we did have to shut down. Bob and I worked during that time, but none of the other employees did. So we scaled back, and it became so much more relaxing. It inspired us to consider doing something other than the grind of the past 32 years.

We were both tired from the stress of the business, but Bob was particularly burned out. He said he could see himself stepping away from the dental chair.

Then in February of 2021, we got a letter in the mail. It was written by a member of Freedom Founders who had been in the exact same situation: burnout after practicing for many years and wanting more freedom of time.

 Freedom
FOUNDERS

519 East IH 30 #246
Rockwall, TX 75087
(972) 203-6960

Dear Robert,

Are you tired of playing the stock market casino during this COVID crisis?

Let's face it, nobody knows when this crisis is going to end.

That means more volatility and uncertainty for your investments and your practice in the days ahead.

So, why continue to "ride it out" and hang your future on the "hope" that the markets cooperate so you can hang up the handpiece and retire comfortably?

That's how I invested for 30+ years. My Dad was a financial adviser and all I knew was "traditional" Wall Street investing.

Over the years, I watched the rules change on my Dad… getting actionable information from inside company boardrooms to make strategic investment decisions became illegal. Slowly, the stock market became a game of chance more than an investing opportunity.

I felt like I was going to a casino and betting on red or black. One day the market was up and I made money. And other days I lost money.

I felt like I was on an endless emotional rollercoaster!

Not only that, but all the money I was socking away in the stock market wasn't helping me become more *free* from my practice in real life.

I was *still* working 12-hour days, including a lot of Saturdays. I was making a lot of money, but I couldn't

see how the stockpile I'd accumulated would EVER create meaningful Freedom of time.

I finally realized that **if you want an extraordinary retirement and _true freedom_ right now, you cannot use** "ordinary" **investments.**

That's what Dr. David Phelps (*a fellow dentist*) taught me. He showed me how to escape the stock market casino and invest in capital investments (*like real estate*) to create cash-flow passive income.

It's really transformed my life. I am no longer chained to my practice and can rest easy knowing that I don't have to depend on Wall Street to reach my financial goals.

Today, the sustainable, predictable cash flow from my investments **has helped me buy back my time.**

The letter made such a deep impression that the next day I called Freedom Founders. After speaking with Dr. Phelps, we joined right then and there—before even attending a meeting.

What gave us hope was that Dr. Phelps had been through what we had been through and found another way. Here was proof that we could do something better than the traditional 401(k), unstable stock market, and endless worry.

"We had been doing this routine all these years. When you go to work when you don't really want to, you get to the point of, *What are we doing?* We were making a good income, but we were in a rut. We needed direction. And luckily, David was there to help us out.

"We had tried other investments over the years. About 30 years ago, we bought a house. It was in a really good location. We were the property managers, cutting lawns and getting phone calls, but

125

I was not a trained property manager. Gertrude and I were doing dentistry, and it just didn't work out. We tried for a couple of years and it just went sour on us, so we gave up on it and sold it at a loss, which was horrible."

We didn't have the guidance or know-how at that age, though we had also made some good investments. My parents have a business that went public, so I bought some stocks in their company. Probably 90 percent of our investments were in the stock market. We were worried if we would have enough money when we retired; we didn't know. We just kept saying, *One more year, one more year...*

But we were thankful to have each other as partners in dentistry. We couldn't have had this career without each other.

"Gertrude and I met at a residency in Fresno, California. I worked as an associate and she started the practice from scratch. We had to borrow from a bank to launch our practice. We tried eight or ten banks before someone would give us money to start. We got hand-me-down equipment and our location was in a poor neighborhood, but we worked ourselves up until we started a new practice in a shopping center.

We rented that for years. Eventually, we purchased that building. It was fun, in a way, starting from nothing in this business. We became productive and profitable. But the game was over. We had done it. Been there, done that. We didn't want to expand anymore. So we tried to find a way out."

After I got injured in 2018, we tried bringing in associates. We interviewed many. We hired one to do root canals, but he only worked one day a week.

"For a year, we looked for someone to hire who could be a part owner. We found someone, but his technique was so bad that we had to let him go. It took me a year and a half to repair all the stuff that he did wrong. It left such a sour taste that we gave up on that.

And we found that associates didn't put in any extra time to make it a practice that we could be proud of. We had created this environment with a great group of employees and patients, and we didn't want to see it go downhill."

So, by our first big group Freedom Founders meeting, we were already members, and we had already had a Blueprint Day with David and Kandace. It was a powerful experience.

"The night before Blueprint Day, there was a large storm and our hotel had lost power. We had half the meeting with no power—just the light of the window! But with or without the light, it was David and Kandace who opened our eyes. We bared our souls and personal finances to them and a couple of other attendees. We just spilled our guts to these strangers—things we don't discuss even with our friends or family—but everyone was so cordial and understanding about our situation. By the end of the meeting, it was spelled out on paper exactly what we needed to do to move forward. It made so much more sense than traditional saving and investing methods. I realized I didn't need to be married to my practice—I could divorce it. That was our goal. David gave us a blueprint and the group gave us a direction. We followed everything he has told us since day one. It's been very, very successful."

Bob had changed his way of thinking prior to Blueprint Day, which made a huge difference. He had wanted to support the ten full-time employees that were working for us. He felt we needed to continue taking care of them, but after talking with David and Kandace, Bob finally realized we didn't need to keep doing that. It was a paradigm shift. Realizing we could sell the practice was another turning point in our thinking.

"It was exciting to realize we had other options that we didn't know were available to us, and that we would have help along the way. David, having gone through it himself, showed that it could be done. He gave us the direction and knowledge to get out of our practice and to rediscover life."

And he wasn't condescending about it because he understood. The integrity showed through. That was big for us.

"He and Kandace sincerely wanted to help and guide us. We didn't see that anywhere else in this profession—dentistry is always trying to get your money. But you could tell David was there to really, really try and help us. The other folks with us on Blueprint Day were all there for similar reasons, but with different needs, and David was trying to make our lives more enjoyable. When we walked out of there that weekend, I was so thrilled that the pressure was off me. There was a way to get out of dentistry and have another way of life. After 36 years of life, there is still time to do other things now, and we're doing it. It's amazing."

When Dr. Phelps was wrapping up with us on Blueprint Day, there was a tear in Bob's eye. The lightbulb had turned on. He said we could sell the practice. It was a defining moment.

"It was overwhelming to take all that money out of the stock market. It was an overwhelming change, but we knew it could work and it was what we needed to do. We did everything they asked us to do right away. Our financial advisor questioned us. It was shocking to people. But we accepted that it was best for us because we believe in David. It just

> **When Dr. Phelps was wrapping up with us on Blueprint Day, there was a tear in Bob's eye. The lightbulb had turned on. He said we could sell the practice. It was a defining moment.**

DRS. GERTRUDE AND BOB DUBANSKI

wasn't working with our financial partners—even if it was a 30-year relationship."

We had meetings with our financial advisors, who said we had enough to retire, but we didn't believe them. What if the stock market went down? It didn't resonate. We couldn't live off what they were suggesting.

"I took out this huge sum of money that I had invested in stock. My family had been involved with that for thirty-some years. I just took it out, which was something that I had really held onto. I felt like I was supposed to keep it. To give that up was really something I never wanted to do. But after talking with David and Kandace, I knew it was the best thing to do. And I'm glad I did it. Now the pie has completely changed. We're now at 90 percent alternative investments. We're at maybe four percent in stock. That 90 percent is now making cash flow."

We have enough for when we do stop working; we're supposed to retire at the end of 2022. We feel comfortable that we have enough passive income to cover our expenses, and that is peace of mind. That's what we've been working for since we joined Freedom Founders. We have enough, plus extra just in case.

It's Time to Sell the Practice

"We agreed on April 21st, 2021, to sell the practice. We put it on the market in July. We found a buyer right away. Unfortunately, it took over eight months to sell it officially because of obstacles between attorneys and brokers. It was really complicated, especially since I was trying to keep the numbers going. I couldn't tell the staff. I wanted the value of the practice to be there by the sale. When we finally sold, it was such a relief. The action items from our Blueprint were actually getting done. The agreement was to keep going until the end of 2022, working a couple of days a week, which is what we're doing. When I go into the office now, I do it because I want to be there. There's no pressure. Working a couple of days is great. Gertrude's now working on a different set of dentistry. She's going to do sleep apnea and TMJ, which is something that was never a possibility before. It's opened up other options."

We don't have any family near us. They have all moved out of California. The only thing keeping us in California was the practice and the office building. Hopefully, we will sell the building to the new practice owner. But as soon as we sold the practice, we started taking trips and seeing family. That was our number one priority. We have the time now.

"My parents live part-time in Reno, Nevada, a couple of hours away from where we live. But I never made the time to visit them much because we had too many things to do. Since selling the practice, my dad must have seen us three or four times in a matter of a month; in the past, it's been three or four times a year! We've traveled to Arizona and to Pennsylvania, to see Gertrude's family. We've got all these plans to finally spend time with our family. The practice was always the excuse to not be able to leave. Now we're free to go."

One thing I have always enjoyed and have the time to do again is running. I did my first 5K in years. Having the time to be in better health makes a big difference in my overall mood. I should have done it earlier. Not having the time is no longer an excuse!

We're still somewhat constrained by the schedule. We still work Monday, Tuesday, and Wednesday, but overall, the schedule is much better than it was.

"We have Thursday through Sunday to go out and do stuff. We never took time off for vacations or long weekends before. It's such a different lifestyle now—I'm a lot more relaxed and I enjoy life so much more. I ride motorcycles. I went fishing on a weekday—that would never have happened before. We've sacrificed all these years. Thinking back to when our son was younger, there were times when he and Gertrude would go on vacations and I couldn't go because of the practice. I had to stay home while they took the week off to see their family. It was a horrible sacrifice.

"We've met so many good people through Freedom Founders. We have group meetings (Freedom Implementation Teams-FIT groups) once a week in addition to the quarterly meetings. I'm generally more of an introvert, but when I go to these meetings, it's such an enjoyable group of people to talk to and listen to. The knowledge they have and the experiences they're willing to share are incredible. We discuss what works for them and what works for us. We work it out together. We generally don't go out with a bunch of dentists. It's just not what we do. At home in California, we just do our work. But meeting fellow dentists in a different atmosphere, in a group of comfortable, happy, relaxed, successful people who are all willing to share—we truly enjoy being with these people. We feel honored. We're all there for the same purpose."

I make it a point to talk to the new members. Not all of us are FIT captains, but we all help in some way.

Recently, I actually got to help by writing a letter similar to the one we received in the mail. I'm hoping the letter will inspire another person to join Freedom Founders like the one that Jim Rachor wrote.

"When new people consider becoming members, you know exactly how they feel because you've been there. I enjoy talking to them, helping them, and inspiring them to know that they are in the right place. It's fun to see people succeed. We all want to help each other. That's the kind of environment David is creating."

I never really loved being a dentist. My parents pushed me into the profession. As a young person, I didn't know what else I could do. So I did it for 36 years. But now, the investments are fascinating to me. I'm happier doing that. It doesn't feel overwhelming or like work. I enjoy it more than dentistry. It's a great new path that I'm very happy to explore; I have a passion for it more so than dentistry. The best way to succeed on a path is if you have an interest in it. It's amazing we did as well as we did in dentistry.

As Bob tells it: "I love dentistry. As a married pair of dentists, in our practice, Gertrude enjoyed the entrepreneurial, business side. There's no way I could have done that. We each stuck to what we did best. It was a partnership that worked very well. We understood that the effort you put into something is what you'll get out of it. So when David told us what we needed to do for our Blueprint, we went gung ho.

"If you really want this to work, you've got to put some effort into it. The work takes around a couple of hours a day—it's not overwhelming. We collaborate on what needs to get done. A husband and wife need to be on the same page because investments are joint decisions. It's hard when just one person does it in the family. Gertrude puts in a couple of hours of work per day to learn, and I learn too. It's like a part-time job. A perk of the job is that we get to meet with Trusted Advisors. We're meeting them in cities across the country that we had never gotten to see before.

"Where else can you meet the people who own the businesses that you're investing in? You never get that kind of opportunity. Freedom Founders is opening the door. It's phenomenal. The rewards are better than working full time. We're in a different state in our lives now—a different state of existence. We're happier than ever because we have time to do things other than dentistry."

The benefit that we can give to a patient from our dentistry is a filling on an upper right molar, for example. But what we're doing with our real estate investments is helping to provide shelter for working people. People always need shelter. We're making money, but we're also helping other people in a bigger way than we could when we were just doing dentistry. I think that's key.

"David gave members' children the opportunity to attend a meeting—to experience what could be possible for their future. Our only child—a son, who is now 26—got so much out of that. The discussions we had with him after the meeting were so much more adult. It's part of our legacy when we leave this world that our son will have this knowledge and share it with his future family. I'm so glad David and Kandace allowed the kids to experience it.

"Right now, we're on our second day of vacation in the beautiful small town of Winnemucca, and we're not thinking about dentistry or our practice. This is our first true vacation since we sold the practice. We have nothing else to worry about. It's an amazing experience after always getting phone calls during time off. It is exactly what we have been needing."

Freedom
FOUNDERS

[First Name],

Are you as burned out in dentistry as I was?

My husband Bob and I were partners in our general practice in Sacramento, California. A few years ago, **I tore tendons in both my wrists while doing surgery.** After that, Bob had to handle the fillings and crowns. Thankfully, he was around to pick up that work, but it showed me just how vulnerable we were.

Bob was toiling in the practice. He became tired of it. <u>On Sundays he would say, *'I don't want to go to work anymore.'*</u> I was afraid he might die in the chair of a heart attack because the stress was so great. I felt like as a wife and business partner I had to do something, but I didn't know what.

For practice owners, current staffing issues are just the tip of the iceberg: There's declining reimbursements, insurance nightmares, personal health problems like mine, and a myriad of other headaches.

We were tied to the practice. It was a monster. We had never even taken a vacation longer than two weeks. We had no alternative sources of income. All we had was what we could produce in our practice. <u>We'd been taught all along to just save money in our 401(k) for some future retirement date,</u> but that wasn't working for us. We had to make some changes now.

I received a letter in the mail from another Freedom Founders member, and it spoke to me. 'That's *exactly* what we need, Freedom.'

GETTING THE BAND BACK TOGETHER
DAVID'S TAKEAWAYS:

For Drs. Bob and Gertrude Dubanski, getting the band back together meant rehearsing a new set after 36 years of playing the same set (dentistry) over and over again. Like so many who, out of default and knowing no other options, put all of their faith in the traditional financial planning model of stocks and 401(k)s, Gertrude and Bob felt that there was no exit from their long and devoted careers in dentistry. When would they have enough? When could they get off the treadmill?

In early 2021, a letter received from a Freedom Founders member prompted them to investigate the community. Dr. Jim Rachor shared his experience with Freedom Founders and how it had created a plan that allowed him to build passive cash flow to replace his active income.

They had tried their hand at real estate investment which did not end well. What they were looking for was a trusted guide and proof of concept—not just the empty promises of a financial planner.

The gamechanger for the Dubanski's came on their Blueprint Day. With a viable plan, they quickly came to the conclusion that they did have enough assets to sell their practice and begin their "next." The decision to sell was made within the next few weeks and a year later, the practice was sold. Their lives were forever transformed.

CHAPTER 13

DRS. PETER AND JANICE FARREHI

My wife, Janice, and I have a special needs son, Luke. He's on the autism spectrum and is now 20 years old. We want to help him achieve a fulfilling life, and hopefully help him find a larger purpose, too. We recognize that we can't be around forever, so we've been exploring some residential options for a larger group of adults with intellectual and developmental disabilities.

To that end, we have joined with several other local families to create a nonprofit. We sit on the board and are exploring options to create a life-sharing community here, inspired by the Innisfree Village community in Virginia. We aim to establish something similar in Ann Arbor, starting from scratch.

The community would be a farm-like atmosphere for adults with intellectual and developmental disabilities. They would live there with caregivers and work the farm for some additional revenue streams. So even someone who may not be able to read or write could still feed the goats, clean out the chicken coop, harvest the eggs, or pick the tomatoes.

In the winter, they could tend to a greenhouse or help with the livestock. It would give individuals a sense of purpose, while at the same time, being a place to live and grow together. If you talk to people who live and work with the intellectually and developmentally disabled community, they are as inspired and educated by the residents with disabilities as they are by anybody else. It's a true spiritual community.

That's what we're called to create, not just to benefit our son, but to benefit a whole community out there looking for residential options. The biggest fear a parent has for their adult child with disabilities is not knowing how they will be taken care of when they are gone or get sick. That's one of the biggest fears we have.

Freedom Founders Has Opened Our Eyes

The group has pushed us to think optimistically that we can and should pursue this now, rather than waiting until we are much older. Plus, the expertise we've developed in real estate investments from Freedom Founders has been a huge help in this endeavor.

I'm a physician, not a dentist. I'm a little bit of a black sheep among the Freedom Founders, although I am definitely a kindred spirit among dentists.

I'm in my mid-50s, and once you get to be my age, you start to see your life as defined by phases with inflection points marking where one phase transitioned into another. By my count, I've had four inflection points in my life so far, the most recent one being when I joined Freedom Founders. But my first inflection point was when I graduated from school and got married.

I grew up in Michigan. I went to college out East and medical school down South, but I'm a Midwesterner at heart. I grew up near Ann Arbor, so I came back to the University of Michigan to finish my graduate and post-graduate work. That's when I met my wife. We fell in love here in Ann Arbor, and we've stayed in Michigan ever since.

My second phase was running my own private practice. I ran my own cardiology practice for ten years. I did the whole thing: hiring and firing people, making payroll, giving raises, running a pension plan, and recruiting associates. But it was difficult to recruit help because there were no palm trees where I lived. Cardiologists were being recruited to milder climates: Fort Worth, Texas; Durham, North Carolina; Arlington, Virginia.

Then, the academic bug bit me. I've always been a teacher. After all, the Latin derivation of the word "doctor" comes from *docere me*, which means "to teach me." At the University of Michigan, I got promoted, my kids graduated from school, and overall, I've found much success. My third inflection point in life was coming back to the Academy, becoming a professor, doing research and administrative work, and providing clinical care.

My fourth was joining Freedom Founders. There was a confluence of several events that led me to Freedom Founders.

The first was a conversation I had with some traditional investors and financial advisors, trying to discern whether to invest in General Motors, Amazon, or a new startup. *How does one decide what to invest in?* I wondered. My advisor finally said, "Sometimes it's just a gut feeling." I thought to myself, "Are you picking stocks or picking *socks?*" There's got to be more to investments than a "gut feeling."

Another incident that led me to Freedom Founders was a casual conversation with a close acquaintance. He asked me what my number was. I had no idea what he meant. He said, "Well, haven't you thought about what the accumulation of your assets needs to be in order to retire?" I had no clue. I thought I would just work until my health wouldn't let me anymore.

The third event was when my brother and I had simultaneous health scares. I recovered, but my brother is permanently handicapped. These three events occurred within six months of one another. It all made me realize, "What if I can't work? How will I support my family and the lifestyle I've come to enjoy?"

My best friend growing up was Dr. James "Jim" Rachor, now one of the longest consecutive-serving Freedom Founders members. He asked me to come to a Freedom Founders meeting. I went and found myself among like-minded people.

I wasn't looking to retire right away; it's a real privilege to be an academic physician. I like being an educator, pursuing knowledge, and training the next generation. After you do it for ten, twenty, thirty, sometimes forty years, you get pretty good at it. Why give up something that you're good at as long your health is in good shape? Most physicians are in generally good health. We try to practice what we preach.

But I did sell my private practice of ten years before my academia journey, and before Freedom Founders was on my radar. It became my nest egg, with 95 percent invested traditionally in growth stocks chosen by a stock picker.

Before Freedom Founders, the only thing that came close to a bad investment happened about a decade ago. I got involved in a startup that went nowhere. A group of local medical professionals each contributed to the LLC. It was a great idea for a product, and we thought it would be the next great medical software. It just didn't pan out. There's such intense competition in the medical software industry.

My initial attraction to Freedom Founders was for diversification outside the traditional equity markets. I knew that I needed a group like Freedom Founders to help with my financial planning and to learn about alternative investments. Jim had given me some books to prepare me for the level of discussion that would take place at the first Freedom Founders meeting.

I couldn't do any of this without my wife, Janice. We're a partnership; we make all our decisions together. On our way to our first meeting, I told her that we didn't have to make a decision on Freedom Founders before we left. "We can go home, reflect on it, and let the group know later if we want to join or not," I said.

But by the second day, she looked at me in all seriousness and said, "We have to join." Once she saw the other couples there and felt that this wasn't some fake group of investors, we were committed. She's totally on board. Although she can't come to every meeting, when she does, she gets a lot out of it.

Mailbox Money Began to Arrive

Soon after joining, I deployed some of my assets and started to see some mailbox money. Because I'm still an employed professional with a traditional retirement plan, I still have some involvement in the stock market, but I quickly deployed to nearly 60 percent in alternative investments.

It ended up being a lot of work on nights and weekends to pursue these alternative investments. It took time to manage, monitor, and report the results of these investments to my accountant. By the time we had our Blueprint Day, I had been in the group for over 18 months.

On our Blueprint Day, Janice told David and Kandace, "You know, Peter is not free because he is spending all of his extra time managing all these investments." We agreed that I needed to expand my real estate investment portfolio to include an executive assistant.

So now I have an executive assistant as a contract employee to help with the paperwork, emails, and bookkeeping. She does everything in QuickBooks, which she provides to my accountant. It saves me a lot of time, and the best part is that it's not virtual: she lives nearby. My wife knows and trusts her. That was a major change that allowed me to spend more time on other things.

As I was approaching my Freedom Number about five years ago, I created a more intentional schedule for myself. I cut back 30 percent at work and then cut back another 20 percent. I gave up a lot of administrative roles initially; I'm not a full-time faculty member anymore. I teach and provide direct patient care, which is the most rewarding part of the job. It's in my DNA, and I see myself still doing it in the future. It was a reduction in pay, but I replaced it with passive income cash flow.

I serve a tremendous population, including the health of my close family and friends. I help them gain access to health care, which is such a vortex in the US. It is very hard to navigate the industry if you don't have someone on the inside. I'm not quite ready to give that up.

I first engaged with Freedom Founders in 2017. A couple more of us joined after my friend Jim: Dr. Andy Baber, Dr. Ben Jensen, and then myself. The four of us have built a lifelong friendship. We talk once a week and have our own unofficial mini group. We help each other with issues big and small, related to our practices, life, and investments. It's been a true God moment to get to know these other fantastic people. Our wives support our friendship and the time that we commit to one another as we figure out the alternative investment world.

Clarity, Purpose and Peace of Mind

I've gained so much more than financial advice from the group: I've regained clarity in my life, my entrepreneurial spirit, and my zest for pursuing new knowledge outside of my profession.

We've been Free for Life™ for about two years. Originally, I thought being Free for Life™ meant hitting that target number. I ended up discovering that it's not a number, but a mindset. I've found clarity in life, a zest for learning, and a willingness to get out of my comfort zone. I've rediscovered my joy of learning, I've built a network of relationships, and most importantly, I have developed a purpose bigger than myself.

Over the past couple of years, I've also found great joy in being a FIT captain. It's rewarding to help dozens of other members in the community, who were like I was just a couple of years ago. I help them stay focused and address their questions and concerns. Creating a legacy within my own family has also helped me pay it forward. For a while, my family did our own FIT calls modeled after the Freedom Founders calls. When two of my older kids moved away, these calls led to some productive family discussions. It allowed me to pass on what I had learned.

I'm still learning a lot every day. I'm interested in learning how to manage people the best way I can. I'm seeing how important good communication skills and relationship building are to my personal growth. Having this freedom to dive deep into relationships through Freedom Founders benefits me, my family, and my higher purpose. I intend to keep focusing on my personal growth and growing the life-sharing community for adults with intellectual and developmental disabilities.

Finding a Greater Purpose

David talks a lot about Maslow's hierarchy of needs. In his version of it, he puts Freedom of Purpose at the top. In many situations, focusing on your professional work can lead to a completely fulfilling life. To be a physician or a dentist, for example, is to provide a service to the public health of your community. But Janice and I focus on a larger purpose beyond ourselves and our professional work. Freedom Founders has allowed us to develop that larger purpose— helping create a community for our son, Luke.

We talk at Freedom Founders about the difference between sequential and simultaneous. Our goal of creating a local living farm community for disabled adults is an example of simultaneous action. This means we're developing this higher purpose while at the same time working on our relationship freedom, our financial freedom, our health freedom, and more. This community is a part of our son's health, so we are helping our family at the same time.

The traditional mindset is sequential: "Oh, I'll deal with that after I retire; after I accumulate so much money; after I step back at work; after my child turns 26." The attitude of Freedom Founders is to recognize that some of these important aspects of our lives require us to work on things simultaneously.

Freedom Founders has given me a roadmap and connected me with a network of other people who are also pursuing excellence in everything that they do. We hold ourselves accountable for the excellence that we are trying to achieve. If you want to be in the top five percent of anything, you're not going to be following the average path. It doesn't come without effort. It's much easier to give more effort when you end up finding achievement or success in your aims, and I have felt that over the last couple of years in being Free for Life™.

GETTING THE BAND BACK TOGETHER
DAVID'S TAKEAWAYS:

Drs. Peter and Janice Farrehi are physicians who joined Freedom Founders at the recommendation of another Freedom Founders member, Dr. Jim Rachor. And it was Janice who said to Peter, "We have to join" after the first day, at their first meeting.

Getting the band back together for the Farrehis encompasses all five of the Freedom Founders' Freedoms: 1. Financial (Freedom Number); 2. Time; 3. Relationships; 4. Health; and 5. Purpose. There is a definitive legacy for the Farrehis in managing and creating a residential community for their son, Luke.

Peter lists his membership in Freedom Founders as one of his key inflection points in life. It has created not only financial freedom, but also lifelong relationships and a mindset that is being passed on to all of their children.

CHAPTER 14

DR. NAREN CHELIAN

I opened my first orthodontics practice a few months *before* I graduated. By working collaboratively with my business partner, we ended up expediting the practice's creation. Because I couldn't practice without a degree, we got our faculty to work for us for a few months while we were finishing up residency. Everything about this plan seemed great, at first—but this was 2008, and soon after we opened, the economy crashed.

With our practice in Las Vegas, my business partner and I ended up getting second jobs a couple of hours away in California. We started working six days a week, going back and forth between two states while trying to hold up our fledgling practice. Two years in, my business partner wanted out, so I bought his share.

Two states, six workdays, five years—it all takes a toll on you. It took about five years before the practice was doing well enough for me to transition out of double duty.

Eventually, I got into a good groove. I started working four days a week. But even though I love what I do, something was missing: I lacked a solid *purpose* in my personal life.

For many, their purpose is their children and spouse. When I was married, I really did feel a sense of purpose with my ex-wife, and for a while, I was in a good place. My work had more meaning when we were together because we shared a life and goals, but it wasn't meant to last.

Just a few months before the COVID pandemic began, our relationship ended. I went from being in the best part of my life personally and professionally to suddenly being lost in my personal life.

It took me about two years to recover from the shock. In some ways, it's still an ongoing process. But one day I woke up with my heart in a better place and asked myself, *"What am I supposed to do in my life now?"*

I enjoyed my life at work. In business for fourteen-plus years, I got the practice to a great place. Working four days a week, my hours were filled as much and as efficiently as possible. I had time to manage meetings, marketing, and strategy with my leadership team. I had time for my patients. But by the weekend, after hitting the work week so hard, my tank was drained. I used the weekends to recharge.

Consuming so much energy meant I had minimal time to rest and also pursue any hobbies, which includes traveling. For years it was a struggle to even spend a week away from my business. I missed out on spending time with friends and family—especially my brothers and my nieces and nephews.

I Lacked Purpose in My Life

And when I got home, I lacked purpose. It was Freedom Founders that helped me find purpose again. Becoming a member marked a huge transition in my post-divorce life.

Before Freedom Founders, I was most proud of my business. We created incredible growth over our first fourteen years. We have a culture and work environment loved by our team; it's fair to say that over 90 percent of the time we're having a blast.

It's a genuinely fun environment, and every one of us feeds off that energy. Even when team members go through hard times, our work environment facilitates a healing process. When you have a hard work environment, the rest of your life is a lot more difficult. But when you go to work and everyone is supportive of you and has your back, you almost feel better. Plus, we're a family business, so we don't work on Saturdays or Sundays. We used to, but when I started taking all weekend off, I soon had my team doing the same.

I recently had craniotomy surgery for a subdural hematoma. It was pretty serious, and I was out for almost six weeks. We were able to get a good network of doctors to cover me for almost two months. Surprisingly, every doctor that worked there said, 'This place is awesome! What you've created here is special." I even had one doctor that wanted to continue working even though he had his own practice! He felt those one or two days would be fun and a great learning experience. Throughout the COVID pandemic and my divorce, work was the best part of my day. Not many people have the luxury to say that.

Then I discovered Freedom Founders. Real estate is something that I've always wanted to get into, but no one seemed to want to share sincerely. Everybody I spoke with seemingly "wanted" to give you something, but when you asked for honest advice, they were shy about it. For some reason or another, any real estate avenue I pursued always fizzled out when I started getting serious about it. The others would hesitate, or not be fully transparent. I don't know if it was selfishness or just a lack of confidence in their own strategy, but whatever the case, I never found it easy to get guidance or partnership in real estate.

I had two good friends in my other mastermind groups that were in Freedom Founders, and as soon as I found out both were in it, I jumped. Sure, it had a big entrance fee, which may preclude someone from joining. And sure, other "advisors" and investment-conscious people in my life told me it was "risky" to have a portfolio of mostly alternative investments. But for me, joining was a no-brainer. To have those who I trust and respect already participating in Freedom Founders was extremely powerful. I had to join.

I had never actually bought a rental. It didn't seem like a good use of my time to buy and fix up a house, then manage it for a tenant. I don't want to go change light bulbs or clean toilets for a hundred bucks a month. It doesn't even make sense. And I didn't know who to trust when it came to property managers, because all you hear are stories of some people doing a great job, some people sucking, and no one who can definitively say "this company is solid."

. . . joining was a no-brainer. To have those who I trust and respect already participating in Freedom Founders was extremely powerful. I had to join.

I could never find others in the real world who did the due diligence I needed. So I just made money, invested it in cookie-cutter mutual funds, and enjoyed my Wall Street-"solid" returns. My approach worked for me, my staff's 401(k), and many practice owners in the dental industry, so I didn't think of making any changes. Set it and forget it, as they say.

Being part of Freedom Founders is like having a true, sincere relationship in which we help each other out, encourage each other, and have each other's backs. When you meet David, it just all comes together because he really wants to help other people with his approach. You instantly get this sense of his sincere desire to help other people. That's powerful, especially because the approach isn't just about the money. We spend just as much time on our relationships, purpose, mindset, and making sure we're headed in the right direction in life.

If you do your homework with Freedom Founders, you can solidify where you stand financially. I'm blessed in that for years I was in the old-school Dave Ramsey mode, where I lived a pretty humble lifestyle, below my means, and didn't get into consumer debt. I accrued wealth and spent cash. I made some traditional investments and kept them going for years.

So, fortunately, I was in a good enough place financially after fourteen years of running my practice. But, of course, I was planning on working the same for the rest of my career until I had "enough" to retire.

Then, on my Blueprint Day, as I went through the numbers with David, I had a welcome shock. I actually did have enough.

To have someone who's as knowledgeable as David look through my numbers and say "You're good" was an incredibly powerful experience. My financial confidence went up significantly. That was the point at which I was finally able to look at myself in the mirror and say, "Now you can run your life and your practice however you want, and you're going to be okay."

In my case, I came in with the assets all ready to be redeployed. I didn't need to accumulate or wait—I was ready to go.

Some new Freedom Founders members invest for growth, and others invest for cash flow. I've discovered that I like a balance between the two. But I will say that in my case and perhaps in that of most other members, I do recommend investing for cash flow at the start. I say this because when I started, I was so excited about investing that I deployed right away into growth and in retrospect, cash flow would've been more fun.

> To have someone who's as knowledgeable as David look through my numbers and say "You're good" was an incredibly powerful experience.

Looking back, I would always invest in cash flow first to get at least a good amount of cash flow coming in. I think securing that cash flow and having that money going to the bank regularly is the ideal route for most members because it increases your confidence in the whole approach. I wasn't stressed about the investments, and the growth returns are great—but it's just more fun to have cash flow coming in regularly to your bank account. It adds to the confidence level you have not just in Freedom Founders, but in your all-around life.

I Love My Work but There's More to Life

I love my work, but there's more for me to love and I want to do it when I'm in my forties, not in my seventies or eighties. I want to travel when I'm healthy. I want to live my life when I'm healthy. I want to do these things while I can.

David has often told us that financial freedom isn't an end-game; it's a new beginning. Once you have financial freedom, you can finally rediscover who you really are. I actually have time now to really look at myself and my life and figure out where best—beyond orthodontics—to devote my resources and energies.

I'm proud to say I got my little brother to become a Freedom Founders member, too. Since joining, my brother and I have actually become much closer. We've spent a lot more time together—at meetings and in between—discussing decisions back and forth and sharing downtime together. Our philosophies have become aligned. It's now at the point where we do family trips together, and these have become the great joy of my life.

We make regular trips now. We just got back from a week at a beach resort in Huntington Beach, CA—my brothers, my parents, my best friend, and all their kids. We all had connected rooms right by the ocean. It was truly magical, and everything a summer vacation should be. We walked the beach in the morning, had heart-to-hearts, and ate good food. That's what freedom is about.

It used to be that we'd just see one another maybe once in the summer and once in the winter. Now we're doing regular trips every other month, which is an incredible amount, and talking a bunch in between. The interactions with Freedom Founders have expedited our relationship even further, to the point where we're making big plans to live in the same state one day.

I'm also much more comfortable with myself in regards to dating and meeting somebody. If I meet somebody, I actually have the time to spend with them now. Freedom allows me to be more myself, to be more present in a relationship, and to enjoy it as it unfolds.

Freedom of time has also rekindled my creativity. My morning routine is important to me, and it's something I refined in my hard-charging early years, so it's at the point where I want to share it with others. I'm in the process of writing a book that will be a useful resource for others in creating a life-defining morning routine.

It's nice to finally have the space to daydream about things that could actually happen. Before freedom, I never had the space to dream up—let alone write—a book. Now I do.

Freedom Creates Confidence

Looking forward, I have confidence in myself and my future. Now I know the direction I'm going in. I don't know where it leads exactly, but I don't have to. I'm just excited that it's going to be somewhere positive.

When you go through a dark time, people always say, "Don't worry, there's light at the end of the tunnel." That's easy to say, but when you're in the tunnel, it's dark and cold. It seems like it could last forever. But there's truth to the statement—there *is* light at the end. Standing in the light, I'm confident that I'm going to be good. The tunnel is behind me.

Today, I look around and see a support system where people are authentically happy for me, authentically there for me, and— if I'm having any struggles—ready for me to lean on. More than ever, I appreciate how awesome and powerful it is to be surrounded by a group of people who sincerely care about me and want me to succeed.

After going through the tunnel, I'm now at a point where I'm excited about rediscovering my purpose. I don't know exactly what it is, but I'm exploring it with Freedom Founders, friends, family, and myself.

I never thought I'd ever be where I am today. Financially, personally, and professionally, every aspect of my life is a blessing. If I knew I'd end up here, I probably would have enjoyed the journey more. If I could go back to my younger self, I would just say, "Hey, you're going to be okay. Enjoy the experience, and don't worry so much about the destination."

The nice house, the best car, the fancy vacations, the "right" spouse and family—I worried too much about these destinations. Now I know these things don't depend fully on my grinding it out, but on my freedom.

Freedom now allows me to enjoy the journey. While the grass may always look greener when somebody else has that one specific thing that you don't have, I now have the confidence to know I'm perfect the way I am. My life is perfect the way I've got it. It's cool that he's got that nice car, that beautiful family, but I'm free from chasing that.

I'm out of the tunnel and in the light, where I can be my authentic self and be fully supported. My purpose, my relationships—I'm excited about everything that's ahead. Most of all, I'm excited that I can finally enjoy the journey.

GETTING THE BAND BACK TOGETHER
DAVID'S TAKEAWAYS:

Dr. Chelian's epiphany came on his Blueprint Day when he discovered that he had all of the investable assets that he needed to create his Freedom Number. All that he needed to do was re-deploy those assets into the proper alternative assets that would create cash flow.

For Naren, getting the band back together is about freedom, travel, family, relationships, and purpose. With the Freedom Founders model, he has the confidence to live his life with complete authenticity—to "enjoy the journey" rather than be stressed because of not knowing how much is enough.

A recent health scare confirmed the blessings of having a business culture of people and colleagues who were all there to support the mission without Naren's direct presence. This event further affirmed his mantra to "live life now" and not to wait for someday.

CHAPTER 15

THE FREEDOM BLUEPRINT DAYS

Expediting a member's "Path to Freedom" begins with the Freedom Blueprint.

A "Blueprint Day" is really a two-day live experience shared with a small (maximum number of six), intimate group of other new members (and spouses where relevant).

In advance, couples complete homework assignments based on our years of serving high-income/high-net-worth couples. This pre-work helps them begin to gain clarity over their definition of freedom, their "why" or purpose, the amount of free TIME they want to create, and by when (the date).

They likewise define non-negotiables—a core value, principle, or conviction that stands above all others. Any other desires or beliefs must yield to these precepts, which may involve areas surrounding family, integrity, time, health and fitness, and personal growth/learning.

Together, we help couples plot their time, money, and meaning goals onto a "Blueprint Map." This process involves assessing and adjudicating current assets and their optimization (or not), along with targeting desired goals and outcomes with specific and measurable milestones.

By the end of the second day, each member/couple has an Action Plan that will carry them through the next ninety days. Clarity and laser focus is the objective of Blueprint Days.

Among the hundreds of couples we have served over the past twelve years, every member/couple completes the Blueprint Days workshop with a feeling of optimism and excitement—a new look at what can be and not what is only wished for.

Community: The Proof Is in the Pudding

A constant theme throughout each story in this book has been community. Trust, authenticity, and friendship are the words used to describe Freedom Founders.

Around any new idea or concept, there is an expectation of fear and skepticism. "If this is so good, why aren't more people doing it or talking about it?" Or, "This must be another sales scheme with trickery and deception!"

But the community shows the truth: the like-mindedness of a curated and high-caliber group who share the same objectives of lifetime freedom, security, and peace of mind removes much of any initial suspicion. The commonality and reassurance of others who have already taken the first steps—and many who have ascended to the summit of freedom—brings a strong sense of confidence even to those who have a difficult time trusting themselves (or their spouses).

FREEDOM FOUNDERS

IDEAL ASSET NUMBER

1. Reverse Engineer
Monthly Expenses *(Before Tax, DOES NOT include current personal debt obligations)* . . . . $ _____
MONTHLY LIFESTYLE BURN RATE

Monthly Payment total for Long Term Debt + $ _____ **6B**
you have kept and are paying down
DEBT OBLIGATIONS

Monthly Debt Equity available from debts paid off, no payments due . . − $ _____ **6A**
INCOME FROM DEBT ELIMINATION

= $ _____ **1A**
MONTHLY BURN RATE

X 12

2. Annualize
Monthly Burn Rate (Lifestyle + Debt) x12 *(Before Tax)*
= $ _____ **1B**
ANNUAL BURN RATE

3. Tax Gross Up
Taxes *(33% gross increase)*
x 1.33

= $ _____ **1C**
ANNUAL INCOME REQUIRED FOR FREEDOM

÷

4. My Rate of Return . . . . . . % ÷ 100 ⟶

= $ _____
INVESTMENT CAPITAL NEEDED

5. Non-Qualified Investing Capital
From your **Capital Organizer** worksheet
− $ _____ **2A**
NON-RETIREMENT FINANCIAL INVESTMENTS

− $ _____ **2B**
CASH ASSETS

6. Total Capital Assets - Retirement
− $ _____ **2G**
RETIREMENT INVESTING CAPITAL

7. Investment Efficiency
Sacrifice...Boat? Vacation home?
− $ _____ **2C**
REAL ESTATE EQUITY

− $ _____ **2D**
OTHER REAL ESTATE EQUITY

− $ _____ **2E**
LIFESTYLE EQUITY

8. Discretionary Capital
Additional capital you are able to save on an annual basis.
− $ _____
DISCRETIONARY CAPITAL

9. Ideal Asset Number
= $ _____
INVESTING CAPITAL GAP

When the Blueprint Is Set, The Rest Is Implementation (Supported by Accountability)

A Blueprint is only an idea until it is followed. Action. Implementation. Forward progress—that's how the Freedom Founders community has been built, on continued guidance and support.

Our community is separated into small pods called "FIT" groups, or Freedom Implementation Teams, of approximately 10–15 members each. Meetings are held weekly over Zoom on different days of the week and at different times to match geographical locations and schedules.

The FIT group meetings follow a cadence or pulse that provides a focal point for accomplishments along with goals and resources for getting to the next step of progress. It is here that deeper relationships are created from the support and accountability that a peer group provides. Many of our members have described the FIT groups as the "glue" that keeps the Blueprint alive.

After conducting hundreds of Blueprint Days, helping high-income professionals create financial game plans for their future, I have observed that there are three stages of wealth-building (remember, *wealth is about TIME and nothing more*):

1. Creating Wealth
2. Protecting Wealth
3. Maintaining Wealth

. . . wealth is about TIME and nothing more.

Initially, creating wealth appears to be the hard part. But that's not true.

The second two stages—protecting and maintaining wealth— require more vigilance, focus, and commitment. Ultimately, the

Freedom Blueprint isn't just about creating cash flow here and now; it's a long-term game. It's about wealth preservation and legacy.

That speaks to the generational aspect our members find so appealing. Legacy is a long-term objective. It's not just here in the moment. It's not just while you're a part of the Freedom Founders community. It's about passing on a specific mindset and resourcefulness to our future generations. Money and wealth are secondary.

What I've Learned from Our Blueprint Days:

- Most participants are closer than they think to their Freedom Number—once they redeploy their capital investments for sustainable cash flow vs. accumulation/depletion models.

- Tax deferral vehicles—401(k), etc.—slow everything down and put capital into a lockbox until age 59.5. The result is lost opportunity and future higher taxation.

- Many highly educated participants possess deep uncertainty and low financial acumen on how to make money work and thus abdicate to Wall Street advisors.

- Gaining an understanding of one's Freedom Number, and the milestones to get there, changes everything—the other four freedoms expand automatically.

- The majority of hardworking business owners miss key financial inflection points and allow market reset/recessions to set them back multiple times over a career.

- Most participants own under-deployed (under-invested) capital due to a lack of knowledge, uncertainty, and known options.

- Many of our members initially exhibit an inability to discuss finances as a couple, which creates a gridlock through which very little progress is ever made.

- Often I encounter a myopic viewpoint of thinking about finances—playing the short game vs. the long game and allowing the tyranny of the urgent to take precedence over future freedom.

- Some participants have a relatively high net worth but no cash flow.

- Most don't know their numbers for both the practice/business and their freedom.

- Many are fearful because there is no vision of "what's next."

Resolving the issues above is the fastest and most direct Path to Freedom.

In Conclusion

In many of our member's stories, I'm sure that you noted how most had tried what I refer to as "Do-It-Yourself" (DIY) investing—in this case specifically in real estate. Several had purchased one or a handful of rental properties. Others had invested in syndications—pooling money through a sponsor-manager. Most of these DIY investing efforts didn't work out well and cost both time and money. They underperformed simply because of "not knowing what you don't know." It was an education in the school of hard knocks.

I, too, started out as an active investor at the age of 22. I had more time–much more time than money–to invest. I had the capacity to learn on my own and could afford to make the common mistakes that beginners will make. It made sense for me to do it this way before I was married, before I had a family, and before my time as a dentist became more valuable.

Active investing may be exactly where you believe you are today. You may not be at a place in your career where you have hundreds of thousands or a million dollars or more to invest "passively." Like I did in my younger years, you are going to have to either take a more active role in your alternative investing or focus on what you can control and optimize–your business or practice–and save until the time is right for you to invest passively.

The downside to active investing is the TIME. If you are single without family responsibilities, you can probably be active in your market to some extent. But learning your market, developing the team and relationships, and gaining some level of expertise is going to pull hard on your time bandwidth. If you are trying to build a business at the same time, you are unlikely to do well with both initiatives. That's my caution to you.

The Freedom Founders Community is focused on those who wish to advocate for their own financial future on a PASSIVE basis. That means no finding properties or investment opportunities, no tenants or contractors, and no toilets. Instead, our community vets and underwrites a diversified group of Trusted Advisors through which our members are able to invest passively and with the social proof of concept. You're never on your own with Freedom Founders.

The ability to earn back one's time is life-changing. As you read in the stories, freedom leads our members to enjoy life anew. After setting aside hobbies and passions during their early, nose-to-the-grindstone working years, sacrificing joys and often a higher purpose, freedom allows them to rediscover *who* they are and *how* they want to spend their time. They can finally turn the heat up on everything in life that had been on the backburner.

If you'd like to gain insights into the Blueprint Day frameworks that I provide for each of our Freedom Founders members, I teach an online, small group, live engagement 4-week course called The 30 Day Blueprint. Whether you want to be active, semi-active or passive, I lay out the key criteria for being successful in any market and exactly what to do and more importantly, what not to do.

If you'd like to be part of the next 30 Day Blueprint, go to www.FreedomFounders.com/30DayBlueprint and we'll put you on our waiting list to notify you of our next dates.

As our members showed you, it's all about time. So, in that spirit, I'll leave you with this: time is no guarantee. So while you still have it, make it a priority.

It's time to rekindle long-dormant joys. It's time to take a fresh direction in life. It's time to get the band back together.

Resources

Whenever you're ready, here are additional ways I can help fast-track you to your journey to freedom of time, money, relationships, health, and purpose.

1. Hear More from Me through Books, Podcast, and Blogs

- *From High Income to High Net Worth: Alternative Investment Strategies to Stop Trading Time for Dollars and Start Creating True Freedom* by Dr. David Phelps, www.HighIncomeBook.com

- *What's Your Next?: The Blueprint for Creating Your Freedom Lifestyle* by Dr. David Phelps, www.FindYourNext.com

- *Own Your Freedom: Sustainable Wealth for a Volatile World*, with Dan S. Kennedy, www.OwnYourFreedomBook.com

- *The Apprentice Model: A Young Leader's Guide to an Anti-traditional Life* by Dr. David Phelps, www.ApprenticeModelBook.com

- *Inflation: The Silent Retirement Killer* by Dr. David Phelps, www.InflationBook.com

- *The Dentist Freedom Blueprint* Podcast, www.DentistFreedomBlueprint.com

- Quick-hitting videos and articles for those looking to jump-start their freedom journey. Visit www.FreedomFounders.com/Blog

2. Schedule a Call with My Team

If you'd like to replace your active income within two to three years, and you have at least $1 million in available capital (can included residential or practice equity and business equity), then go to the following link to schedule a call with my team: www.FreedomFounders.com/Schedule

3. Get Your Free Retirement Scorecard

Benchmark your retirement and wealth-building against hundreds of other practice professionals and business owners. Get personalized feedback on your biggest opportunities and leverage points. Go to www.FreedomFounders.com/Scorecard to take the three-minute assessment and get your scorecard.

4. Receive My Monthly Newsletter: Path to Freedom

Get "inside access" to the strategies used by hundreds of dentists, doctors, and practice professionals to create a combined *millions of dollars of passive income*. This publication is packed with strategies, principles, and techniques. It's an easy 30-minute read that will expand your mind and unlock wealth-building potential to catapult you from high income to high net worth. Mailed every month it's a power-packed resource. **www.PathToFreedomNewsletter.com**

5. Work with Me Directly

If you'd like to work directly with me and a small group of my closest investment colleagues, with direct access to the dealmakers and asset classes that I invest in, message me at **admin@FreedomFounders.com** and put "Fast Access" in the subject line, or call (972) 203-6960 (ext. 160) and leave a brief message. Let us know you're interested in the Fast Access program—we'll set up a time with you to talk, find out about your goals, and see if there's a fit.

6. Access Special Bonus Items:

www.RediscoveringYourLifeResources.com

7. Register For My Next 30-Day Blueprint

Whether you are new to real estate investing and trying to begin or you have invested in a few deals but know there are things you need to learn, this class is for you. It's an online, small group class full of live engagement over a 4-week period. Go to **www.FreedomFounders.com/30DayBlueprint**

About the Author

DR. DAVID PHELPS

Who is Dr. David Phelps?

And why should you listen to him?

A Practice Owner Turned CEO and Leader

David owned and managed a private practice dental office for over 21 years before his daughter's health crisis served as a dramatic wake-up call in his life. David's "Plan B" (a portfolio of cash flow producing real estate assets) gave him the Freedom to sell his practice mid-career and focus 100% on what matters most to him.

David does not follow the majority but lives life and does business on his own terms and is not dictated to by others.

America's #1 Authority on Creating Freedom in Life and Business

David is the author of seven published business, finance, and success books. As a nationally recognized keynote speaker, David brings dynamic energy and unique insights into how to create financial freedom through passive income, how to build a real business that doesn't take over your life, anti-traditional real estate investing, private lending, wealth-building legacy, and how to take responsibility and "own" your life.

A Leader Born through Crisis

Sitting with his daughter in the hospital room after her battle with leukemia and a life-saving liver transplant, Dr. David Phelps realized what matters most. It was not his career as a dentist that had consumed his daily life for over 21 years. He needed to be present for his daughter, Jenna.

He decided he would no longer practice dentistry. Instead, he was able to pivot to his Plan B.

He drew inspiration from his years of investing avidly in real estate that began during his time in dental school with a joint-venture investment with his father. By leveraging the lessons and capital he had acquired, David built an investment portfolio that could generate enough passive income to leave his dental practice and be the father his daughter needed.

An Escapee of the Dollars-For-Hours Trap

David's radical new life intrigued his peers, who asked him how they too could command control of their wealth and time. By bringing together his two worlds—high-income medical professionals and real estate professionals—David created a powerful network of like-minded professionals who could support each other on their own paths to financial and personal freedom.

He called this group Freedom Founders, and as its leader, he found his purpose: helping his colleagues break the chains of bondage to their practices and financial fears and create freedom in their lives.

With his own life as proof, David challenges the traditional model of wealth building, which preaches abdicating control over one's money to advisors and entrusting all of one's investing capital to Wall Street.

David has witnessed too many high-income professionals blindly trust the traditional path only to have their hard-earned wealth wiped out by the volatility of the public market. Through Freedom Founders, David exhorts his members to take back control of their investing capital from their practices and 401(k) plans, put it to work in more stable, capital-producing assets like real estate, and always stay focused on their own freedom.

Free for Life™

Freedom Founders Mastermind Group began as a meeting of sixteen people over a decade ago and has grown into a community of over 100 members and Trusted Advisors, where David's insights into the financial markets, alternative investing, and achieving success and fulfillment in life attract freedom-seeking members from across the country.

Speaking from his own experience (David is the "product of the product"), David strives to instill in his members the courage to lead lives unhindered by the expectations of others and driven by purpose. Following in his footsteps, Freedom Founders members attain the tools to become Free for Life™: they can live entirely on the passive income from their real estate investments.

A Recognized Leader in Dentistry and Real Estate

David has been featured in Advantage ForbesBooks, The Profitable Dentist, Dental Success Today, The Progressive Orthodontist, MarketWatch, Business Insider, Markets Insider, Value Investing News, Morningstar, Yahoo! Finance, and *Entrepreneur* magazine, among others. He has been awarded the GKIC Marketer of the Year (2011) award.

He regularly keynotes and presents at live events, and has co-hosted multiple virtual and webinar conferences. He is frequently asked to guest present at niche industry mastermind meetings.

David regularly collaborates with countless industry leaders including Dr. Dustin Burleson, Dr. David Maloley, Dr. Michael Abernathy, Dan Sullivan, Steven J. Anderson, Scott Manning, Alastair Macdonald, Dr. Scott Leune, Jason Medley, Shaun McCloskey, Eddie Speed, Daniel Marcos, Christopher Ryan, Dr. John Meis, Dr. Christopher Phelps, and countless others.

At his own events, he has shared the stage with Garrett Gunderson, Chuck Blakeman, Adam Witty, Dr. Dustin Burleson, Dr. David Moffet, Dr. David Maloley, Mike Michalowicz, Tony Rubleski, Jim Palmer, Thomas Blackwell, and many others.

An Expert in the World of Real Estate

David's expertise in the world of real estate includes everything from multi-family apartments, self-storage, commercial properties, mobile home parks, retail properties, single-family rentals, structured notes, private debt, managed funds, and more. He has successfully weathered multiple market corrections—notably using the 2006–2008 downturn to successfully more than double his net worth.

He is regularly consulted in the creation, structure, and economics of large multi-investor syndications, funds, and private investments secured by real estate assets.